9th SIGHAN Workshop on Chinese Language Processing 2017

Taipei, Taiwan
1 December 2017

ISBN: 978-1-5108-5289-1

Printed from e-media with permission by:

Curran Associates, Inc.
57 Morehouse Lane
Red Hook, NY 12571

Some format issues inherent in the e-media version may also appear in this print version.

Printed by Curran Associates, Inc. (2017)

For permission requests, please contact the Association for Computational Linguistics at the address below.

Association for Computational Linguistics
209 N. Eighth Street
Stroudsburg, Pennsylvania 18360

Phone: 1-570-476-8006
Fax: 1-570-476-0860

acl@aclweb.org

Additional copies of this publication are available from:

Curran Associates, Inc.
57 Morehouse Lane
Red Hook, NY 12571 USA
Phone: 845-758-0400
Fax: 845-758-2633
Email: curran@proceedings.com
Web: www.proceedings.com

SIGHAN-9

The 9th SIGHAN Workshop on Chinese Language Processing

Proceedings of the SIGHAN-9 Workshop

December 1, 2017
Taipei, Taiwan

Introduction

The 9th SIGHAN Workshop on Chinese Language Processing (SIGHAN-9) at IJCNLP 2017, December 01, 2017, Taiwan

Growing interest in Chinese language processing is leading to the development of linguistic corpora and automatic tools. As more resources have become available recently, it is crucial to create a platform that allows easy exchange of information and data and the comparison of different approaches to various NLP tasks. Among about 20 SIGs within the Association for Computational Linguistics, SIGHAN (Special Interest Group on Chinese Language Processing) provides an umbrella for researchers in industry and academia working in various aspects of Chinese language processing. SIGHAN workshop provides an international forum for both researchers and practitioners to report their latest innovations, summarize state-of-the-art in the field, as well as exchange ideas, results, and visions in all aspects of Chinese language processing.

The previous SIGHAN workshop series were started in 2002. SIGHAN-1 was held in conjunction with COLING-02 (Taipei, Taiwan); SIGHAN-2 was held in conjunction with ACL-03 (Sapporo, Japan); SIGHAN-3 was held in conjunction with ACL-04 (Barcelona, Spain); SIGHAN-4 was held in conjunction with IJCNLP-05 (Jeju Island, Korea); SIGHAN-5 was held in conjunction with ACL-COLING-06 (Sydney, Australia); SIGHAN-6 was held in conjunction with IJCNLP-08 (Hyderabad, India); SIGHAN-7 was held in conjunction with IJCNLP-13 (Nagoya, Japan) and SIGHAN-8 was held in conjunction with ACL-IJCNLP 2015 (Beijing, China).

The purpose of the SIGHAN-9 is to identify challenging problems facing the development of Chinese language processing systems, and to shape future research directions through the publication of high quality, applied and theoretical research findings. We encourage submissions of papers on all topics in the general areas related to computational linguistics and speech/text processing of Chinese natural languages.

Organizers:

Yue Zhang, Singapore University of Technology and Design
Zhifang Sui, Peking University

Program Committee:

Jie Yang, Singapore University of Technology and Design
Jiangming Liu, University of Edinburgh
Yu Yuan, Singapore University of Technology and Design
Yuze Gao, Singapore University of Technology and Design
Yanxia Qin, Harbin Institute of Technology
Shuailong Liang, Singapore University of Technology and Design
Deng Cai, Shanghai Jiao Tong University
Chenhua Chen, Singapore University of Technology and Design

Invited Speaker:

Yue Zhang, Singapore University of Technology and Design
Wanxiang Che, Harbin Institute of Technology

Table of Contents

Conference Program

[8:00-9:00] *Chinese Segmentation and POS-tagging Leveraging Heterogenous Corpora*
Yue Zhang (**Invited talk**)

[9:00-9:25] *Group Linguistic Bias Aware Neural Response Generation*
Jianan Wang, Xin Wang, Fang Li, Zhen Xu, Zhuoran Wang and Baoxun Wang

[9:25-9:50] *Neural Regularized Domain Adaptation for Chinese Word Segmentation*
Zuyi Bao, Si Li, Weiran XU and Sheng GAO

[9:50-10:15] *The Sentimental Value of Chinese Sub-Character Components*
Yassine Benajiba, Or Biran, Zhiliang Weng, Yong Zhang and Jin Sun

[10:15-11:00] *Coffe break*

[11:00-12:00] *Syntactic and Semantic Parsing*
Wanxiang Che (**Invited talk**)

[12:00-12:25] *Chinese Answer Extraction Based on POS Tree and Genetic Algorithm*
Shuihua Li, Xiaoming Zhang and Zhoujun Li

[12:25-12:50] *Learning from Parenthetical Sentences for Term Translation in Machine Translation*
Guoping Huang, Jiajun Zhang, Yu Zhou and Chengqing Zong

Group Linguistic Bias Aware Neural Response Generation

Jianan Wang[1], **Xin Wang**[2], **Fang Li**[1], **Zhen Xu**[2],
Zhuoran Wang[3] and **Baoxun Wang**[3]
[1]Shanghai Jiao Tong University, Shanghai, China
[2]Harbin Institute of Technology, Harbin, China
[3]Tricorn (Beijing) Technology Co., Ltd, Beijing, China
[1]{wangjianan,fli}@sjtu.edu.cn
[2]{xwang,zxu}@insun.hit.edu.cn
[3]{wangzhuoran, wangbaoxun}@trio.ai

Abstract

For practical chatbots, one of the essential factor for improving user experience is the capability of customizing the talking style of the agents, that is, to make chatbots provide responses meeting users' preference on language styles, topics, etc. To address this issue, this paper proposes to incorporate linguistic biases, which implicitly involved in the conversation corpora generated by human groups in the Social Network Services (SNS), into the encoder-decoder based response generator. By attaching a specially designed neural component to dynamically control the impact of linguistic biases in response generation, a Group Linguistic Bias Aware Neural Response Generation (GLBA-NRG) model is eventually presented. The experimental results on the dataset from the Chinese SNS show that the proposed architecture outperforms the current response generating models by producing both meaningful and vivid responses with customized styles.

1 Introduction

Automated Chat Agents (a.k.a chatbots) have drawn great attention in Natural Language Processing research in recent years (Shang et al., 2015; Li et al., 2016; Wu et al., 2016; Xing et al., 2017), and the springing up of the practical chatbots (e.g., Duer[1], XiaoIce[2], etc.) indicates the great potential of such systems for naturally connecting human beings with various online services.

The core functionality of chatbots is to interact with users for the purpose of general conversation. This requires chatbots to generate responses not only relevant to users' queries but also in accordance with users' preferred talking styles (Allwood et al., 1992). State-of-art practical chatbots are capable of providing basic chatting functionality with necessary task-oriented abilities. However, they all lack the capability of adapting the generated responses to meet users' preferences. To improve the user experience, it is necessary to add such talking style customization function in these chat agents. In previous studies, **inter-group linguistic biases** are observed and found in daily conversations among people from different communities (Maass et al., 1989). In this paper we generalize such biases into those among groups of people based on their profiles or social attributes. People from different groups may have different talking styles, including syntactic (sentence structure), semantic (choice of words) or even attitudinal differences. Then such challenge of chatbots could be defined as: how to express such differences in the generated responses for different user preferences.

Benefiting from the nature of the Deep Neural Networks (DNN) based encoder-decoder framework (Sutskever et al., 2014), previous studies tried to jointly learn the representation of each **individual's talking habits** in the training procedure of word embedding, and take such habits as a part of the input to generate personalized responses (Li et al., 2016; Alrfou et al., 2016). It is found that, given a large amount of high-quality utterance data of each user, this methodology can obtain promising results of personalized response generation. For practical chat agents, however, it is not trivial to collect such high-quality utterance from users. As a consequence, it is observed that the expected responses to similar queries tend to

[1]http://duer.baidu.com/
[2]http://www.msxiaoice.com/

Proceedings of the 9th SIGHAN Workshop on Chinese Language Processing, pages 1–10,
Taipei, Taiwan, December 1, 2017. ©2017 AFNLP

be uncharacteristic, that is, the effect of individual-level personalized response generator is not significant. Therefore, it is more reasonable to generate personalized responses by modeling the feature of a group of users, rather than an individual (Hu et al., 2014).

Query	What are you doing?
Group A	I am watching a **basketball game**.
Group B	I am **shopping** on Amazon!
Query	I uninstalled your game just now.
Group A	How could you do that!
Group B	You are so dead.

Table 1: Responses from two user groups (A & B) categorized by user gender. The examples are selected from the real Chinese Social-Network-Service (SNS) dataset and translated into English.

In real world data, it is observed that the distinct features of generated responses are generally reflected by keywords and sentence structures, as shown in Table 1, which matches previous findings. Therefore, in order to leverage the group linguistic biases in an encoder-decoder based model, we need to apply such biases in the process of word generation. The model should be capable of controlling the distribution of such biases, rather than assigning equal intensities on each word in the response. This could make the generated responses distinguishable in groups of people in the distinctiveness of keywords and sentence structures while still guaranteeing the validity of the sentence both on semantic and syntactic level. This could thus prevent the generated responses similar on structure and use of words.

In this paper, we propose an encoder-decoder based architecture, Group Linguistic Bias Aware Neural Response Generation (GLBA-NRG) model, which incorporates **linguistic biases of human groups** into an encoder-decoder based response generator, in order to tackle the talking style customization problem of practical chatbots. We attempt to learn the representations of the linguistic biases from a gender-split corpora. Such representations are then used to bias the word selection in the response generation process. More importantly, we present a specially designed neural network component, as a soft-switch to conduct the dynamic controlling of the impact of linguistic biases on each generation step. With the adoption of the linguistic bias impact controlling mechanism, our model is able to generate responses highly corresponding to the specified talking style, while the semantic relevance between queries and responses is well maintained.

The rest of this paper is organized as follows: Section 2 surveys the related work. Our proposed model is detailed in Section 3. Section 4 describes the experimental setups and analyzes the results. Finally, our work is concluded in Section 5.

2 Related Work

Along with the development of Neural Machine Translation(NMT), many recent studies show that the basic neural-based encoder-decoder framework (Sutskever et al., 2014; Bahdanau et al., 2014) can also be successfully applied in conversation modeling (Vinyals and Le, 2015; Yao et al., 2015; Zhou et al., 2016; Iulian et al., 2017), which generates a response on the basis of a given query. Based on the work of Vinyals and Le (2015) that directly applies sequence-to-sequence (Seq2Seq) architecture for response generation, Shang et al. (2015) introduce the global and local scheme with attention signal into the generation of response, while Sordoni et al. (2015) take contextual information into account to generate context-sensitive responses.

Besides the query and contextual information, several explicit and implicit factors (e.g. topic, emotion) play great roles in response generation. To utilize such factors for generating informative, diverse and interesting responses, several works incorporate topics, external knowledge, emotional content, and responding mechanism into conversation models. Xing et al. (2017) and Xu et al. (2016) extract related topics or knowledge from the query and context respectively, then add these info into conversational models, so as guiding them to generate informative and interesting responses. Ghosh et al. (2017) and Zhou et al. (2017b) explore the influence of the affective information in response generation with Affect-LM and emotional memory separately. Taking explicit and implicit factors as the high-level semantic content of the response, Serban et al. (2017) and Zhou et al. (2017a) propose latent variable and responding mechanism respectively to enrich the capability of conversation models to generate diverse responses.

Moreover, the personality is of great importance for chatbots to respond coherently, as argued by Vinyals and Le (2015). The very first attempt to model persona is from Li et al. (2016),

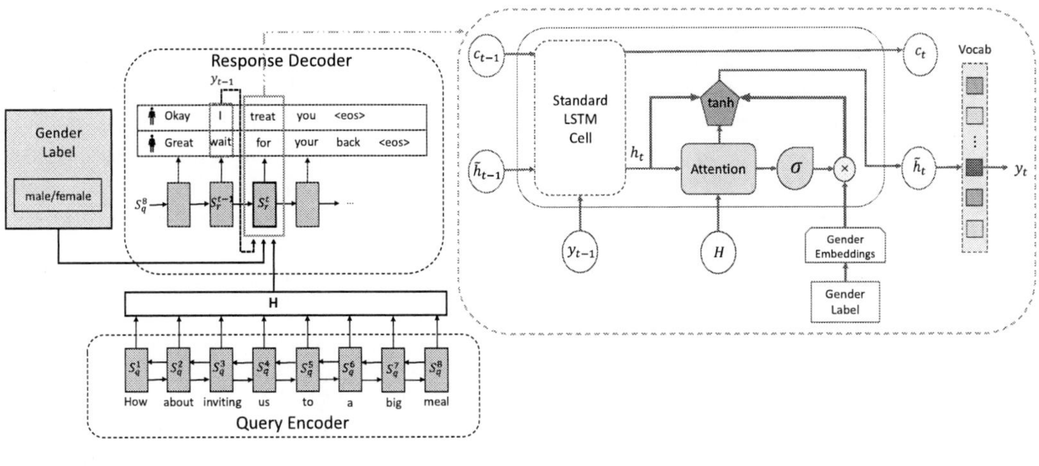

Figure 1: Architecture of our Group Linguistic Bias aware Neural Response Generator (GLBA-NRG).

who propose to encode speaker-specific information and conversation style with user embeddings to influence each generation step. In contrast to launch persona in response generation from individual view (Li et al., 2016), this paper explores to endow chatbots with language styles from the human group aspect.

3 Learning to Generate Linguistic Biased Responses

In this section, we will first formalize the problem, then present the model overview, and finally describe the encoder and decoder architecture of GLBA-NRG.

3.1 Problem Formalization

Our goal is to train an encoder-decoder based model M to generate the response $r = \{y_1, y_2, \cdots, y_j\}$ conditioned on an input query $q = \{x_1, x_2, \cdots, x_n\}$ and the pre-defined **user group label** gl, that is, the training target is to maximize the conditional probability $p(r|q, gl)$. Here, the group label indicates the linguistic biases in the user generated contents.

3.2 Model Overview

Inspired by the research work of Schwartz et al. (2013), who point out that the difference of word distribution of distinct groups is revealed by a few words usage, this paper aims at exploring a mechanism for introducing the linguistic bias into response generating models, and meanwhile controlling the impact of this factor in the generation of each word. They also point out that gender is the most distinguishable feature to split human groups, and thus we take responses from males and females respectively as the corpus for demonstrating our idea. According to the work of Li et al. (2016), it is reasonable to represent users with special embeddings in Seq2Seq based models. This paper follows this set-up by learning the gender embedding g_v and integrating it into our framework.

In our model, a standard Bi-LSTM is taken as the encoder to represent the query q. In this process, the output of the Bi-LSTM is fed into the decoder for response generation. Unlike the decoding procedure in classic Seq2Seq model, we introduce a specially designed neural component to attach to the decoder. This neural component works as a soft-switch gate, converting the attention results based on the hidden layer outputs into a scalar ranging from 0 to 1. Taking the scaled gender embedding and the attention output as parts of inputs, the decoder conducts general steps to generate responses. Figure 1 illustrates the architecture of the proposed response generator.

Our model enjoys several advantages comparing with current response generators. On one hand, through the newly introduced neural component, the linguistic bias information could be adopted into the encoding-decoding process and thus the linguistic biases of different human groups are integrated to the response generation process effectively. On another, our model is able to pick the keywords that reflect different language styles by dynamically control the impact of the linguistic bias in each generating step. Due to such advantages, our model is expected to generate vivid responses to queries.

3.3 Encoder

As is shown in Figure 1, a query $q = \{x_1, x_2, \cdots, x_n\}$ is fed into the encoder of our model, and projected to a representation vector $H = [h_1^q, \cdots, h_i^q, \cdots, h_n^q]$, where

$$h_i^q = \begin{bmatrix} \overrightarrow{h_i^q} \\ \overleftarrow{h_i^q} \end{bmatrix} \quad (1)$$

The encoding process of the query by bidirectional LSTM (Schuster and Paliwal, 1997) is detailed as follows. First, the forward states $\left(\overrightarrow{h_1^q}, \cdots, \overrightarrow{h_n^q}\right)$ are computed:

$$\begin{bmatrix} i_t \\ f_t \\ o_t \\ l_t \end{bmatrix} = \begin{bmatrix} \sigma \\ \sigma \\ \sigma \\ \tanh \end{bmatrix} \overrightarrow{W} \begin{bmatrix} \overrightarrow{h_{t-1}^q} \\ e_t \end{bmatrix} \quad (2)$$

$$\overrightarrow{c_t} = f_t \odot \overrightarrow{c_{t-1}} + i_t \odot l_t \quad (3)$$

$$\overrightarrow{h_t^q} = o_t \odot \tanh(\overrightarrow{c_t}) \quad (4)$$

where i_t, f_t and o_t indicate the input gate, memory gate and output gate respectively, $e_t \in \mathbb{R}^{1\times m}$ denotes the word embedding for an individual word at time step t, $\overrightarrow{h_t^q} \in \mathbb{R}^{|q|}$ denotes the vector computed by the LSTM model at time t, $\sigma(\cdot)$ is the logistic sigmoid function, and $\overrightarrow{W} \in \mathbb{R}^{4|q|\times(m+|q|)} = \left[\overrightarrow{W_i}, \overrightarrow{W_f}, \overrightarrow{W_o}, \overrightarrow{W_l}\right]$. $\odot$ denotes the element-wise multiplication.

The backward states $\left(\overleftarrow{h_1^q}, \cdots, \overleftarrow{h_n^q}\right)$ are computed similarly. We share the word embedding between the forward and backward LSTMs.

3.4 Group Linguistic Bias Aware Decoder

Basically, with the query representation H inherited from the encoder, our proposed methodology aims at building a decoding mechanism $f(\cdot)$ that is able to systematically adopt both the query semantics and the Group Linguistic Bias (GLB) to generate responses. Formally, this decoding mechanism can be described by the following Equation:

$$\tilde{h}_t = f(h_t, H, e^g) \quad (5)$$

where e^g denotes the dense vector (a.k.a, embedding) representing the human group g and this embedding is designed to imply the group linguistic bias. h_t is the hidden state of the decoder at time step t, and $\tilde{h}_t$ can be taken as an updated hidden state integrated with group linguistic bias. Based on $\tilde{h}_t$, the decoding process follows:

$$p(y_t = w|q, g) = softmax(W_v^\top \tilde{h}_t) \quad (6)$$

where $p(y_t = w|q, g)$ indicates the output word distribution at time step t, and W_v is the weight matrix of the output layer.

The major motivation for proposing the GLBA decoding mechanism is to make the impact of such linguistic bias controllable in the generation of each word in responses. As stated in Schwartz et al. (2013), different human groups differs in use of words in general and thus we can take advantage of such distinct and specified words. Therefore, a model that is capable of highlighting such distinct words for different groups could express group differences effectively.

In this part, we define the specified decoding mechanism $f(\cdot)$ as

$$f(h_t, H, e^g) = W_f[h_t, a_t, e^g \odot g_t] + b_f \quad (7)$$

where W_f and b_f denote the NN related weights and biases respectively. Especially g_t indicates a neural gate transferring the attention outputs upon H into a scalar, so as to control the impact of e^g by performing the element-wise multiplication represented by $\odot$. The operations within the gate g_t can be described by:

$$g_t = \sigma(W_g a_t + b_g) \quad (8)$$

where W_g and b_g denote the weight and bias respectively.

Noticing that Equation 7 and 8 have taken the attention result denoted by a_t, the attention mechanism is formalized as follows:

$$a_t = \textstyle\sum_{j=1}^{T} \alpha_{tj} h_j \quad (9)$$

$$\alpha_{tj} = \frac{\exp(e_{tj})}{\sum_{k=1}^{T_x} \exp(e_{tk})} \quad (10)$$

$$e_{tj} = W_a[h_t, h_j] + b_a \quad (11)$$

The reason for introducing attention model into the gate is that, intuitively, the impact of the linguistic bias (represented by the group embedding) on the response words is determined by the semantic of the corresponding query, that is, based on the content of a query, our model is expected to locate the essential words in the response to apply a stronger impact of linguistic bias.

For decoding, the N-best lists are generated using the decoder with beam size B=30. We set a maximum length of 30 for the generated candidates. At each time step of the decoding process, we first examine all $B \times B$ possible next-word candidates, and add these next-word probabilities up to the corresponding hypothesis' joint probability, which contain all the previous words' probabilities in a certain hypothesis. After that, the candidate words are sorted by their joint probabilities and pick out the new top-B unfinished hypotheses and move to the next word position. If any hypothesis meets an *EOS* token, this hypothesis will be added to the result set as one of finished response.

4 Experiments

4.1 Data Preparation

For validating the capability to integrate group linguistic bias into response generation of our model, the dataset should possess group attributes. Therefore, we collected data from one of Chinese real-name social network sites (SNS), in which some utterances have explicit group attributes (e.g. gender, age, etc). We obtained about 240,000 sessions with multi-turn conversations and user profiles from the SNSs. We filtered out potential advertisements, forwards and non-original utterances (including queries and responses), and only kept Chinese words, English letters and digits in each utterance. After the above preprocessing, there are about 5 million query-response pairs remained. The number of words (sequence length) of query or response ranges from 1 to 30.

Each query-response pair has 4 parts of basic information $\langle q, q_u, r, r_u \rangle$, where q is a query, r is the response corresponding to q, and q_u or r_u indicates user ID who posted the query or response. If the profile of r_u is accessible from his or her home page, we tagged the query-response pair with *group linguistic label* obtained from r_u's profile. According to the *group linguistic label*, the 5 million query-response pairs were split into two subsets: one subset includes 4 million pairs without *group linguistic label*, the other is composed of about 1 million labeled pairs. We take the 4 million pairs to pre-train the models, and the details will be given in Subsection 4.3. For the 1 million labeled pairs that used in group linguistic bias experiments, we firstly sampled 2,000 labeled pairs as testing data, and then sampled training and validation data from the remaining pairs. The sizes of training and validation sets are illustrated in Table 2.

Train	male	483,228
	female	482,915
Valid	male	8,052
	female	8,091

Table 2: Data Description

Notice that there is no overlap among pairs in training, validation, and testing sets.

4.2 Baselines

We consider the following baselines in our experiments.

S2S: the standard Seq2Seq model (Sutskever et al., 2014; Bahdanau et al., 2014).

GLBA-Static: to verify the effectiveness of the gate in GLBA-NRG, we keep the attention module but remove the gate which is specially designed to weight gender embeddings. Thus, the attention module only contributes to the output, with no effect on the gender embeddings. The gender embeddings are injected into the decoder as their weights equal 1.0. This baseline is an variant of our GLBA-NRG model. It should be noted that, the GLBA-Static model is **equivalent** to the speaker model proposed by (Li et al., 2016).

For the sake of comparison, we rename our GLBA-NRG model as GLBA-Dyna in order to distinguish from GLBA-Static.

4.3 Training Protocols

Pre-Training: The 4 million query-response pairs **without group label** were utilized to pre-train the basic Seq2Seq model, to initialize the LSTM parameters including baselines and our approach. This is based on the following considerations:

- To obtain better word embeddings benefiting from a bigger dataset, which is trained from random initialization;
- To accelerate convergence in the following experiments since parameters are initialized by a raw Seq2Seq conversation system (Erhan et al., 2010);

The S2S, GLBA-Static and GLBA-Dyna all follow the training protocols below: 1) the encoder is a 2-layer Bi-LSTM network with 1,000 hidden cells for each layer; 2) the decoder is a 1-layer unidirectional LSTM network with 1,000 hidden cells; 3) the batch size is set to 128; 4) use Adam optimizer with a fixed learning rate 0.0001; 5) parameters are initialized by sampling from the uniform distribution [-0.1, 0.1]; 6) gradients are clipped to avoid gradient explosion with a threshold of 1; 7) the vocabulary size is limited to 100,000; 8) the dimensions of word and gender embeddings are both 500.

In our experiments, S2S, GLBA-Static and GLBA-Dyna use the same dataset, which consists of 1 million query-response pairs **with gender labels** (no overlapping with the 4 million query-response pairs for pre-training). The details of train/valid splitting are described in Table 2. Notice that when applying the dataset in S2S, we only use query-response pairs and ignore group labels.

4.4 Evaluation Methods

According to (Liu et al., 2016), the perplexity and BLEU metrics are not suitable for evaluating the response generators, although they are widely used in translation evaluation. Hence, we only use the human judgement in our experiment.

We recruit 3 annotators for human evaluation. The annotators are instructed to judge responses from 2 aspects, response quality and accuracy.

Response Quality: The response quality refers to whether a response is appropriate and attractive to the input query. Three levels are assigned to a response with scores of 0, +1, +2:

- **Attractive (+2)**: the response is evidently a vivid and informative response to the query;
- **Neutral (+1)**: the response is plain and general but suitable to the query;
- **Unsuitable (0)**: it is hard or impossible to find a scenario where the response is suitable.

To make the annotation task operable, the suitability of generated responses is judged from the following four criteria:

(a) **Grammar and Fluency**: Responses should be natural language and free of any fluency or grammatical errors;

(b) **Logic Consistency**: Responses should be logically consistent with the test query;

(c) **Semantic Relevance**: Responses should be semantically relevant to the test query;

(d) **Vividness**: Responses are vivid and information-rich but should not contradict the first three criteria;

If any of the first three criteria (a), (b), and (c) is contradicted, the generated response should be labeled as "Unsuitable". The responses that conform to the first three criteria (a), (b), and (c) but general or flat should be labeled as "Neutral". The responses that completely satisfy the four criteria (a), (b), (c), (d) should be labeled as "Attractive".

Accuracy: Besides the measure of response quality, we also consider whether a response corresponds to its expected group category (as input to the model). For GLBA-NRG models (GLBA-Static and GLBA-Dyna), we ask the annotators to provide a rating score 0, 1 for the judgement.

S2S, GLBA-Static and GLBA-Dyna generate $B = 30$ responses separately using the beam search algorithm described in Section 3.4. Responses generated by different models are pooled and randomly shuffled for each annotator.

4.5 Results & Analysis

Table 3 shows an overall evaluation by calculating the average score of the generated responses. It is clear that GLBA-Dyna outperforms the baseline models, whose average score is up to 1.404, while others' scores are both below 1.0. This means that the responses generated by GLBA-Dyna are grammatical and query-relevant, and also possess vividness which is crucial for making chatbots attractive to users.

Method	Average Score
S2S	0.923
GLBA-Static	0.944
GLBA-Dyna	**1.404**

Table 3: Average Score of Human Evaluation.

Table 4 details the human evaluation scores of generated responses from all approaches in this paper. Compared with S2S, GLBA-NRG models (GLBA-Static and GLBA-Dyna) achieve higher scores on responses labeled as "+2", especially GLBA-Dyna. This phenomenon demonstrates that GLBA-NRG models generate more vivid and informative responses. The improvement on vividness is ascribed to the group linguistic bias of GLBA-NRG models.

Method	Score		
	0	+1	+2
S2S	14.56%	78.56%	6.88%
GLBA-Static	17.56%	70.50%	11.94%
GLBA-Dyna	**8.22%**	**43.11%**	**48.67%**

Table 4: Human annotation results for **responses quality**. The grade evaluation criteria is described in detail in Section 4.4.

As illustrated in Table 4, in contrast to S2S, GLBA-Dyna increases 41.79% on "+2" responses and reduces 35.45% on "+1" ones, while GLBA-Static achieves ~5% improvement on "+2" responses. Since both GLBA-Static and GLBA-Dyna introduce the group linguistic features as inputs, this phenomenon is ascribed to the different strategies of controlling group linguistic biases. That means the proposed mechanism biasing the general S2S probability distribution is more effective for incorporating the linguistic features, which renders the responses vivid. On one hand, the proposed mechanism dynamically explore possible positions for keywords that implied gender, on the other hand, it is dynamically aware of which keyword is suited in such a position. Under this mechanism, GLBA-Dyna could select out lively and cute words to make responses vivid.

All models have a proportion of unsuitable responses (labeled as "0") ~10% but GLBA-Static generates more bad responses (17.56%). After checking its bad responses, we find that GLBA-Static tends to generate swear words for most queries as male, and tends to generate "Uh Hmm" for most queries as female. This observation could be ascribed to the fact that the GLBA-Static model takes the external bias (as the gender embedding) as an input augmentation in every time-step of response generation without dynamic switch. Since only the keywords in one response need such external bias to demonstrate the group distinction, it's unwise to apply external bias in the whole process of response generation. In other words, overweighted group bias excessively intervene in the word distribution when decoding, which leads to less correlation between the response and query. Therefore, the responses from GLBA-Static have no much remarkable variation in the quality compared with S2S.

To validate the capability of our model on generating group linguistic biased responses, this paper evaluates whether the gender inferred from the generated response is consistent with the predefined gender label. Table 5 illustrates the evaluation results.

Method	Accuracy
S2S	-
GLBA-Static	0.340
GLBA-Dyna	0.493

Table 5: Gender Consistency Results.

It can be seen that the proposed model GLBA-Dyna achieves 49.3% on accuracy, which indicates that half of the responses generated by GLBA-Dyna are consistent with the input gender linguistic bias. Comparing with the 34.0% accuracy of GLBA-Static, our model GLBA-Dyna is more effective on controlling the gender linguistic bias in response generation. The reason is that GLBA-Dyna moderates the gender embedding information and dynamically regulates three factors' weights, current hidden state of decoder, query context and gender embeddings, to produce more suitable and reasonable responses. Instead, GLBA-Static deactivates the gate so it can not control the external bias spontaneously.

4.6 Case Study

As is shown in Figure 2, S2S could generate responses relevant to queries but very few of them is appealing to users since basically they are acknowledgements of the queries and do not make any new points to interact with the users. In comparison, the responses generated by both GLBA-Static and GLBA-Dyna are more interesting while keeping the relevance with the queries. We find that GLBA-Dyna generates responses with richer information, compared with GLBA-Static. More importantly, GLBA-Dyna responses exhibit prominent distinction of language styles between males and females, on both semantic and syntactical level. We believe this attributes to the gender distinction aware dynamic switch mechanism in GLBA-Dyna decoder.

In Figure 3, we visualize the gender gate of each time-step in response generation, to illustrate the dynamic controlling process of the gender distinction in GLBA-Dyna model. The different shades of red reflect the degrees of the gate activation. It can be seen that the gender gate is strongly activated in the position where the keywords in-

Query	Model		Reponse(Original)	Response(Translated)
我这早零下了。 It has been below zero degrees for long.	S2S		我这零下十几度。	It is around minus 10 degrees here.
	GLBA-Static	Female	可怜的孩纸。	Poor child...
		Male	这么冷。	That is so cold.
	GLBA-Dyna	Female	这么冷啊， 我们还没开始穿羽绒服呢。	Wow that is so cold. We do not even need to wear down jackets here.
		Male	这么冷，注意保暖。	That is so cold. Keep warm.
OKOK，俺还想晚上麻将。 OK. I would really like to play Mahjong tonight.	S2S		我也想啊，想你们啊。	I would like to do so. I really miss you.
	GLBA-Static	Female	好的好的，等你回来。	Yeah let us play it once you are back.
		Male	来吧，哥。	Yeah let us do it, dude.
	GLBA-Dyna	Female	好滴好滴， 等你回来， 我们一起去玩。	That is great! We can play it together once you are back.
		Male	来吧，热烈欢迎， 哥招待你。	Yeah let us do it bro. Do you wanna play it at my place?
生病好难受啊， 健康的时候一定要快快乐乐的， 好好珍惜。 It feels so bad to get ill. We should cherish the life when we are healthy.	S2S		嗯哪。	Yeah it is.
	GLBA-Static	Female	嗯嗯，谢谢亲爱的。	Thank you, darling.
		Male	恩，谢谢关心。	Thanks for asking.
	GLBA-Dyna	Female	嗯嗯，知道了， 亲爱的。	Ok I see, my dear.
		Male	恩，谢谢兄弟关心啊。	Thanks for asking, dude.

Figure 2: Cases selected from the testing set.

Query	Gender	Response									
我这早零下了。	Female	这么	冷	啊	我们	还	没	开始	穿	羽绒服	呢
	Male	这么	冷	注意	保暖						
OKOK，俺还想晚上麻将。	Female	好滴	好	滴	等	你	回来	我们	一起	去	玩
	Male	来	吧	热烈欢迎	哥	招待	你				
生病好难受啊，健康的时候一定要快快乐乐的，好好珍惜。	Female	嗯	嗯	知道	了	亲爱	的				
	Male	恩	谢谢	兄弟	关心	啊					

Figure 3: Gate activation of each time step by GLBA-Dyna.

fer gender distinguishable information. The fact that the gate value of the same word varies with gender label corroborates the effectiveness of dynamic gate activation. In other words, our gate is able to use gender information to control the response generation.

5 Conclusion

In this paper, we have presented a group linguistic bias aware neural response generation model, so as to tackle the talking style customization problem in chatbot implementation. The contributions of our work can be summarized as follows.

a) Instead of modeling and adopting the language style of each individual, this paper proposes to learn the linguistic biases of human groups and introduce such biases into the response generator, which makes the style in responses more explicit and reliable;

b) We have designed a special neural component that is able to dynamically control the impact of the introduced group linguistic bias in each generation step, to select the keywords reflecting language styles, rather than rigidly enforcing linguistic bias for each word.

References

Jens Allwood, Joakim Nivre, and Elisabeth Ahlsén. 1992. On the semantics and pragmatics of linguistic feedback. *Journal of semantics* 9(1):1–26.

Rami Alrfou, Marc Pickett, Javier Snaider, Yunhsuan Sung, Brian Strope, and Ray Kurzweil. 2016. Conversational contextual cues: The case of personalization and history for response ranking .

Dzmitry Bahdanau, Kyunghyun Cho, and Yoshua Bengio. 2014. Neural machine translation by jointly learning to align and translate. *arXiv preprint arXiv:1409.0473* .

Dumitru Erhan, Yoshua Bengio, Aaron Courville, Pierre-Antoine Manzagol, Pascal Vincent, and Samy Bengio. 2010. Why does unsupervised pre-training help deep learning? *Journal of Machine Learning Research* 11(Feb):625–660.

Sayan Ghosh, Mathieu Chollet, Eugene Laksana, Louis-Philippe Morency, and Stefan Scherer. 2017. Affect-lm: A neural language model for customizable affective text generation. *arXiv preprint arXiv:1704.06851* .

Liang Hu, Jian Cao, Guandong Xu, Longbing Cao, Zhiping Gu, and Wei Cao. 2014. Deep modeling of group preferences for group-based recommendation. In *AAAI*. volume 14, pages 1861–1867.

Vlad Serban Iulian, Klinger Tim, Tesauro Gerald, Talamadupula Kartik, Zhou Bowen, Bengio Yoshua, and C. Courville Aaron. 2017. Multiresolution recurrent neural networks: An application to dialogue response generation. In *Proceedings of the Thirty-First AAAI Conference on Artificial Intelligence, February 4-9, 2017, San Francisco, California, USA.*. pages 3288–3294.

Jiwei Li, Michel Galley, Chris Brockett, Georgios Spithourakis, Jianfeng Gao, and William B. Dolan. 2016. A persona-based neural conversation model. In *Proceedings of the 54th Annual Meeting of the Association for Computational Linguistics*.

Chia-Wei Liu, Ryan Lowe, Iulian V Serban, Michael Noseworthy, Laurent Charlin, and Joelle Pineau. 2016. How not to evaluate your dialogue system: An empirical study of unsupervised evaluation metrics for dialogue response generation. *arXiv preprint arXiv:1603.08023* .

Anne Maass, Daniela Salvi, Luciano Arcuri, and Gün R Semin. 1989. Language use in intergroup contexts: the linguistic intergroup bias. *Journal of personality and social psychology* 57(6):981.

Mike Schuster and Kuldip K Paliwal. 1997. Bidirectional recurrent neural networks. *IEEE Transactions on Signal Processing* 45(11):2673–2681.

H Andrew Schwartz, Johannes C Eichstaedt, Margaret L Kern, Lukasz Dziurzynski, Stephanie M Ramones, Megha Agrawal, Achal Shah, Michal Kosinski, David Stillwell, Martin EP Seligman, et al. 2013. Personality, gender, and age in the language of social media: The open-vocabulary approach. *PloS one* 8(9):e73791.

Iulian Vlad Serban, Alessandro Sordoni, Ryan Lowe, Laurent Charlin, Joelle Pineau, Aaron C Courville, and Yoshua Bengio. 2017. A hierarchical latent variable encoder-decoder model for generating dialogues. In *AAAI*. pages 3295–3301.

Lifeng Shang, Zhengdong Lu, and Hang Li. 2015. Neural responding machine for short-text conversation. *Computer Science* .

Alessandro Sordoni, Michel Galley, Michael Auli, Chris Brockett, Yangfeng Ji, Margaret Mitchell, Jian-Yun Nie, Jianfeng Gao, and Bill Dolan. 2015. A neural network approach to context-sensitive generation of conversational responses. *arXiv preprint arXiv:1506.06714* .

Ilya Sutskever, Oriol Vinyals, and Quoc V Le. 2014. Sequence to sequence learning with neural networks. In *Advances in neural information processing systems*. pages 3104–3112.

Oriol Vinyals and Quoc Le. 2015. A neural conversational model. *arXiv preprint arXiv:1506.05869* .

Bowen Wu, Baoxun Wang, and Hui Xue. 2016. Ranking responses oriented to conversational relevance in chat-bots. In *COLING 2016, 26th International Conference on Computational Linguistics, Proceedings of the Conference: Technical Papers, December 11-16, 2016, Osaka, Japan*. pages 652–662.

Chen Xing, Wei Wu, Yu Wu, Jie Liu, Yalou Huang, Ming Zhou, and Wei-Ying Ma. 2017. Topic aware neural response generation. In *Thirty-First AAAI Conference on Artificial Intelligence*.

Zhen Xu, Bingquan Liu, Baoxun Wang, Chengjie Sun, and Xiaolong Wang. 2016. Incorporating loose-structured knowledge into conversation modeling via recall-gate lstm .

Kaisheng Yao, Geoffrey Zweig, and Baolin Peng. 2015. Attention with intention for a neural network conversation model .

Ganbin Zhou, Ping Luo, Rongyu Cao, Fen Lin, Bo Chen, and Qing He. 2017a. Mechanism-aware neural machine for dialogue response generation. In *Thirty-First AAAI Conference on Artificial Intelligence*.

Hao Zhou, Minlie Huang, Tianyang Zhang, Xiaoyan Zhu, and Bing Liu. 2017b. Emotional chatting machine: Emotional conversation generation with internal and external memory. *arXiv preprint arXiv:1704.01074* .

Xiangyang Zhou, Daxiang Dong, Hua Wu, Shiqi Zhao, Dianhai Yu, Hao Tian, Xuan Liu, and Rui Yan. 2016. Multi-view response selection for human-computer conversation. *EMNLP16* .

Neural Regularized Domain Adaptation for Chinese Word Segmentation

Zuyi Bao and **Si Li** and **Weiran Xu** and **Sheng Gao**
Beijing University of Posts and Telecommunications, Beijing
baozuyi,lisi,xuweiran,gaosheng@bupt.edu.cn

Abstract

For Chinese word segmentation, the large-scale annotated corpora mainly focus on newswire and only a handful of annotated data is available in other domains such as patents and literature. Considering the limited amount of annotated *target* domain data, it is a challenge for segmenters to learn domain-specific information while avoid getting over-fitted at the same time. In this paper, we propose a neural regularized domain adaptation method for Chinese word segmentation. The teacher networks trained in *source* domain are employed to regularize the training process of the student network by preserving the general knowledge. In the experiments, our neural regularized domain adaptation method achieves a better performance comparing to previous methods.

1 Introduction

As the Chinese text comes without word delimiters, the Chinese word segmentation becomes a necessary step towards further syntactic analysis. With the evolving of statistical word segmentation techniques (Peng et al., 2004; Kiat Low et al., 2005; Zhang and Clark, 2008), some of the state-of-the-art systems (Sun, 2011; Hatori et al., 2012) reported high accuracy in large-scale annotated dataset (Xue et al., 2005; Emerson, 2005). However, as large-scale annotated corpora mainly focus on domains like newswire, it often brings a significant decrease in performance when we directly apply models trained on these corpora to other domains (Liu and Zhang, 2012; Li and Xue, 2014; Qiu and Zhang, 2015). Such a problem is mainly due to the differences in distributions between the training (source domain) and testing (target domain) data, and well-known as *domain adaptation*. In this paper, we focus on the fully-supervised domain adaptation (Daume, 2007) where large-scale annotated corpora of source domain and only a handful of annotated data of target domain are available. As the annotated data in target domain is often insufficient to train a effective model, the key problem is how to fully explore the information contained in the target domain data and avoid getting over-fitted at the same time.

Regularization is often employed in previous domain adaptation methods to escape the trap of over-fitting. Blitzer et al. (2007); Rozantsev et al. (2016) introduced loss functions that prevent corresponding weights from deviating significantly from the source model parameters. Kullback-Leibler divergence was added to force the feature distribution from adapted model to be close to that from the unadapted model (Yu et al., 2013). Ganin et al. (2016) adopted adversarial training to ensure that the feature distributions over the different domains are close to each other. In this paper, we employ a neural regularized domain adaption method based on *Knowledge Distillation* (Bucilu et al., 2006; Hinton et al., 2015) for Chinese word segmentation.

Knowledge distillation is first designed and proposed to do model compression (Bucilu et al., 2006; Hinton et al., 2015), where a teacher model and a student model is involved. The teacher model is a complex model and trained on large-scale annotated data. The student model is a small model and trained by mimicking the output of the teacher model. Because knowledge distillation is able to transfer knowledge between models, this method is extended and applied to other tasks. Li and Hoiem (2016) adopted this method to gradually add new capabilities to a multi-task system. Hu et al. (2016) transferred the knowledge of first-

Proceedings of the 9th SIGHAN Workshop on Chinese Language Processing, pages 11–20,
Taipei, Taiwan, December 1, 2017.

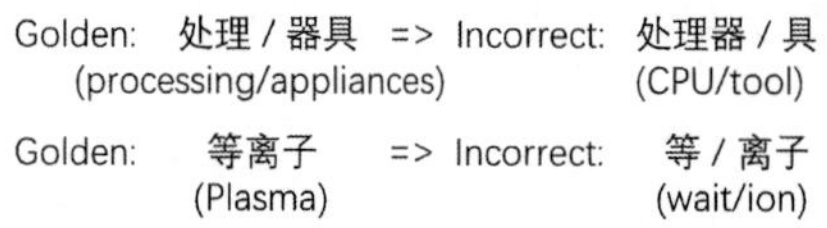

Figure 1: The model trained on newswire data makes mistakes on patent data.

order logic rules to enhance neural networks.

Domain adaptation is also explored by using knowledge distillation. Ao et al. (2017) utilized the unlabeled data to transfer the knowledge from the source models. Support Vector Machine is used as base classifier to efficiently solve the imitation parameter. Ruder et al. (2017) employed a measure for obtaining the trustworthiness of a teacher model. However, previous work mainly focus on semi-supervised domain adaptation of sentiment analysis, while we explore the fully-supervised domain adaptation of Chinese word segmentation.

In the domain adaptation for Chinese word segmentation, two kinds of domain adaptation tasks have been explored. One is annotation standard adaptation (Jiang et al., 2009; Chen et al., 2017), which explores the common underlying knowledge between the corpora with different annotation standards. The other is document type adaptation (Liu and Zhang, 2012; Liu et al., 2014; Zhang et al., 2014; Qiu and Zhang, 2015; Li and Xue, 2016), such as using newswire document to label novel (Liu et al., 2014).

In this paper, we focus on the document type adaptation which is a challenging problem in many real-world applications. As shown in Fig. 1, the model trained on publicly available newswire data outputs incorrect segmentation for patents.

In the previous work of this task, lexicons were proved effective for improving cross-domain performance (Zhang et al., 2014; Liu et al., 2014). Cross-domain features were explored to capture the characteristics of distributions utilizing unlabelled data in both source and target domain (Liu and Zhang, 2012; Li and Xue, 2016). However, previous methods mainly focus on feature-based methods utilizing unlabelled data or external resources such as lexicons. How to utilize a handful of annotated target domain data is still under exploration.

In this paper, we propose a neural regularized domain adaption method for Chinese word segmentation. A neural segmenter trained with source domain data is employed as the teacher model. A student model is then trained with target domain data under the regularization from the teacher model. The regularization retains the general information from source domain and prevents the student model from over-fitting during the target domain-specific training. Our contributions are as follows:

(1) we propose a neural method for fully-supervised domain adaptation of Chinese word segmentation and show its effectiveness in the experiments.

(2) we perform our neural domain adaptation method with different hyper-parameters and show it works as an neural regularization.

(3) we analyse the results showing that our method explores the domain-specific information and preserves the general knowledge at the same time.

(4) we propose a split of CTB9 data and perform domain adaptation experiments on the CTB9.

2 Method

2.1 Fully-supervised Domain Adaptaion

In the fully-supervised domain adaptation of Chinese word segmentation, one or multiple source domains $\{D_{s_1}, \cdots, D_{s_i}\}$ are provided with one target domain D_t. In each source domain, a trained model T_i or a large-scale of annotated sentences $\{(x_1, y_1), \cdots, (x_{n_i}, y_{n_i})\}$ are available. While only a handful of annotated target domain sentences $\{(x_1, y_1), \cdots, (x_{n_t}, y_{n_t})\}$ are provided, where we have $n_i >> n_t$. In the domain adaptation, we aim at training a model that works well on the target domain. As the amount of target domain annotated data is limited, we are forced to explore both the general information of the source domain and the domain-specific information of the target domain.

2.2 Baseline Segmenter

In this paper, we take the convolutional neural segmenter as our baseline model because that (1) same as previous baseline models, convolutional neural segmenters take Chinese word segmentation as sequence labelling task (Xue, 2003); and (2) previous baseline segmenters (Liu and Zhang, 2012; Zhang et al., 2014; Li and Xue, 2016) are limited with local features. Therefore, it may be unfair to take recurrent networks with long-range dependence as rival; (3) the performance of convolutional neural segmenter is comparable with previous baseline segmenters.

The architecture of our baseline model is simplified from (Chen et al., 2016), we remove the highway, recurrent and k-max pooling layer. And it is equivalent to a feed-forward neural network (Collobert et al., 2011) with multiple window sizes. We take the convolutional neural segmenter as an example, but our method is not limited by the architecture of neural segmenters.

The basic unit of convolutional neural networks (CNN) is filters (Kim, 2014), a filter of window size w is represented as $\mathbf{m} \in R^{w \times d}$ where d is the size of embeddings. Let $\mathbf{x}$ refers to the concatenate of w character embeddings. Then features $\mathbf{c_i}$ from a filter i is generated by:

$$\mathbf{c_i} = f(\mathbf{m} \otimes \mathbf{x} + \mathbf{b}), \tag{1}$$

where $\otimes$ is convolution operator, $\mathbf{m}$ and $\mathbf{b}$ are the weight matrix of filter and bias, f is the non-linear function such as ReLU in our network. And for each window size, multiple filters are applied to generate multiple feature maps which are concatenated together. Then a softmax layer is appended for predicting the label of each character. Our neural word segmenter regards Chinese word segmentation as a sequence labelling task. The segmenter adopts BIES (Begin, Inside, End, Single) four labels scheme which represents the position of character inside a word. During the training phase, the cross-entropy cost function is used. And during the testing phase, the label sequences are constructed through beam search.

2.3 Neural Regularization

As shown in Fig. 2, the architecture of our neural regularization strategy consists of a teacher network and a student network. Both of them can be arbitrary neural network structures, and we take our baseline segmenter as an example. The teacher network can be obtained in two ways: (1) a provided source domain segmenter; or (2) a segmenter trained by provided annotated source domain data. And we aim at utilizing the teacher network $softmax(f_T(x))$ with a handful of target domain data $(x_1, y_1), \cdots, (x_{n_t}, y_{n_t})$ to train a student network $softmax(f_S(x))$ that works well in target domain.

The process of training is as following: (1) a sentence is feeded into the teacher network and the soft label distribution of each character s^T is predicted by the teacher network as:

$$s_{ij}^T = softmax(f_T(x_{ij})/T), \tag{2}$$

where x_{ij} is the j-th character of i-th sentence, T is a hyper-parameter named temperature to control the smoothness of the soft label distribution and smooth the regularization. (2) similar with step 1, the sentence is also feeded into the student network. The label distribution p^S and a smoothed version s^S are predicted for each character by the student network as:

$$p_{ij}^S = softmax(f_S(x_{ij})), \tag{3}$$
$$s_{ij}^S = softmax(f_S(x_{ij}/T)), \tag{4}$$

(3) train the student network with the annotated target domain data using the loss function as:

$$\ell_{seg} = \frac{1}{n}\sum_{i,j} -y_{ij} \log p_{ij}^S, \tag{5}$$
$$\ell_{re} = \frac{1}{n}\sum_{i,j} -s_{ij}^T \log s_{ij}^S, \tag{6}$$
$$\arg\min_{\theta} \ell = \alpha \ell_{seg} + (1-\alpha)\ell_{re}, \tag{7}$$

where ℓ_{seg} is the supervised loss, ℓ_{re} is the regularization loss from the teacher network, θ is the parameters in the student network, α is a hyper-parameter balancing the supervised loss and regularization. Our neural regularization for Chinese word segmentation can be easily applied to multiple source domain scenario as:

$$\ell_{seg} = \frac{1}{n}\sum_{i,j} -y_{ij} \log p_{ij}^S, \tag{8}$$
$$\ell_{re_m} = \frac{1}{n}\sum_{i,j} -s_{ij}^{T_m} \log s_{ij}^S, \tag{9}$$
$$\arg\min_{\theta} \ell = \alpha_1 \ell_{seg} + \sum_m \alpha_m \ell_{re_m}, \tag{10}$$
$$s.t.\ \alpha_1 + \sum_m \alpha_m = 1, \tag{11}$$

where ℓ_{re_m} is the regularization loss from the m-th teacher network. The amount of target domain data is insufficient to train a model that generalizes well directly. In our neural regularized method, the neural regularization loss from the teacher network prevents the student network from overfitting in the target domain and protects the general information from the domain-specific training.

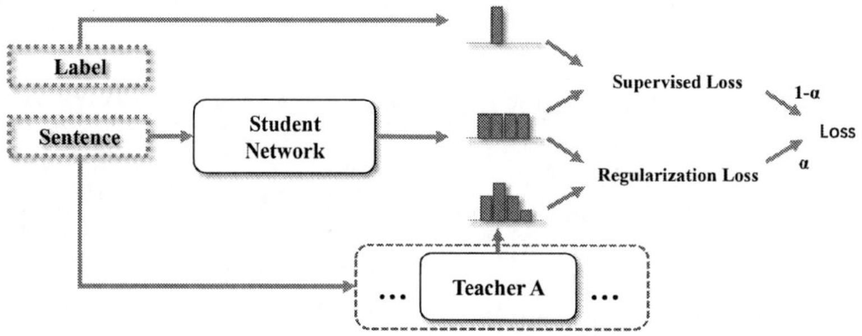

Figure 2: The architecture of our neural regularization strategy for the domain adaptation of Chinese word segmentation.

Our neural regularization is different from the traditional regularization used in the domain adaptation such as weights regularization (Blitzer et al., 2007; Rozantsev et al., 2016). The weights regularization works as a global setting that prevents any weights deviating from source domain models. Our neural regularization is more meticulous and tunes the loss of each sample respectively.

Type	Sec.	Source		Target	
		CTB5	CTB7	Patent	Zhuxian
sent.	train	18k	36k	11k	2.4k
words.		641k	839k	345k	67.6k
sent.	dev.	0.35k	4.8k	1.5k	0.79k
words.		6.8k	120k	46.2k	20.4k
sent.	test	0.35k	11k	1.5k	1.4k
words.		8.0k	241k	48.4k	34.4k

Table 1: Statistics of source and target datasets

Type	Sec.	CTB9			
		nw	wb	sc	cs
sent.	train	8.1k	8.3k	35.2k	12.7k
words.		197k	167k	242k	124k
sent.	dev.	1.1k	0.80k	4.3k	1.9k
words.		26.5k	21.3k	30.6k	17.6k
sent.	test	1.1k	1.1k	4.5k	2.1k
words.		26.7k	21.7k	30.6k	18.9k

Table 2: Statistics of genres used in our experiments. nw refers to *Newswire*. wb, sc and cs refer to *Weblogs*, *SMS/Chat messages* and *conversational speech*.

3 Experiments

3.1 Dataset

Following previous Chinese word segmentation domain adaptation methods, we employ the Chinese Treebank (CTB) (Xue et al., 2005) as the source domain data. The Patent (Li and Xue, 2014) and Zhuxian (Zhang et al., 2014) are used as the target domain data. The patent is often a description of a specifically designed system, which contains a high concentration of technical terms. Zhuxian is a Internet novel and has a different writing style comparing to CTB. Zhuxian also contains many novel specific named entity. The statistics of the data is shown in Table 1. It is obvious that the amount of source domain data is much larger than target domain data.

We also perform our method between different genres of CTB9. The *Newswire* (nw) in CTB9 is chosen as the source domain data. The *Weblogs* (wb), *SMS/Chat messages* (sc) and *conversational speech* (cs) are employed as the target domain data. We split each genre into train, development, test set, and the filelist is shown in Table 3. The statistics of the data is shown in Table 2. Note that in the CTB9, the source domain nw is not significantly larger than target domain such as wb, cs. The nw is even smaller comparing to sc.

3.2 Hyper-Parameter Settings

In the experiments, the hyper parameters are chosen through grid search. The filters are set to 300 feature maps for each window size ranging from 2 to 5 characters. A dropout of 50% is adopted. The size of unigram and bigram character embeddings is 200 with a 20% dropout.[1] The training is done through stochastic gradient descent with Adadelta (Zeiler, 2012). The hyper-parameter T is set to 2. The α is set to 0.4 for *Zhuxian 300s* and CTB9 *Weblogs*, 0.5 for *Patent 10*, 0.6 for CTB9 *conversational speech*, *Zhuxian 600s* and *Patent 20*, 0.7 for *Patent 100*, 0.8 for CTB9 *SMS/Chat messages*

[1]We use the bigram embedding following the implements of (Zhang et al., 2016).

Genres	Sec.	ID list
nw	dev.	4041-4045, 0924-0927, 0830-0857, 0531-0535, 0443-0448, 0254-0288.
	test	4046-4050, 0928-0931, 0858-0885, 0536-0540, 0449-0454, 0289-0325.
wb	dev.	4332-4336.
	test	4337-4411.
sc	dev.	6548-6623.
	test	6624-6700.
cs	dev.	7014-7015.
	test	7016-7017.

Table 3: The split filelist of each genre. We only list the filelist of development and test data. The rest of data in each genre is used as training data.

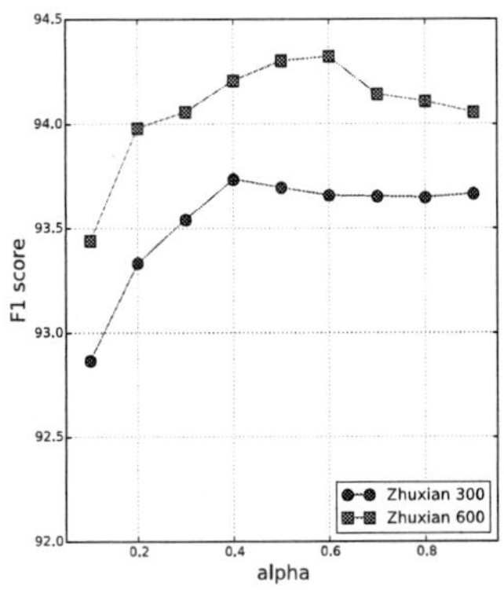

Figure 3: The results of our neural regularized method under different hyper-parameter α in Zhuxian development data.

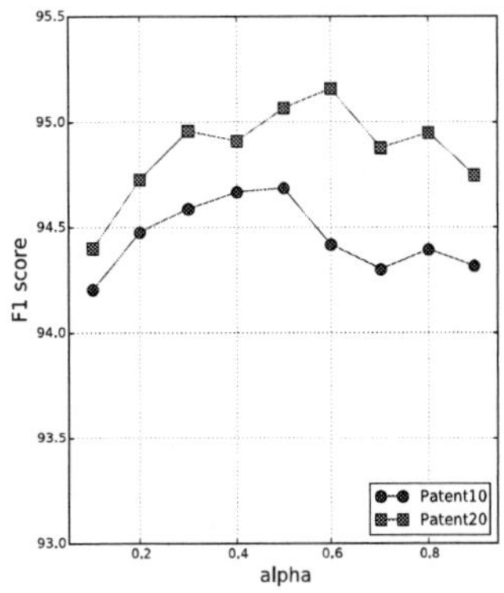

Figure 4: The results of our neural regularized method under different hyper-parameter α in Patent development data.

according to the performance on the development set. [2] The beam size of beam search is 10. We pre-train the embeddings using the publicly available Chinese Wikipedia corpus with *word2vec*. The teacher network and student network share the same architecture and hyper-parameter setting for simplicity.

3.3 Regularization Weights

For the traditional weight regularization, a hyper-parameter is often included to control the degree of regularization. When the network is regularized heavily, it often leads to under-fitting. While slight regularization may lead to over-fitting. In this section, we employ experiments to explore the effectiveness of the balancing hyper-parameter α used in our neural regularization. We want to know how the hyper-parameter α influences the performance of our method.

We perform our method in experiments between both CTB5 to Zhuxian and CTB7 to Patent. The hyper-parameter settings of the segmenter is same as mentioned in Sec. 3.2. The hyper-parameter α is searched ranging from 0.1 to 0.9 with a step size of 0.1. The results of CTB5 to Zhuxian and CTB7 to Patent are shown in Fig. 3 and Fig. 4.

Take CTB5 to Zhuxian as an example, we train our teacher network with training data from CTB5 and perform our neural domain adaptation method to a student network using *Zhuxian 300s* and *Zhuxian 600s*. For both *Zhuxian 300s* and *Zhuxian 600s* data, the performance of our student network first improves and then decreases with the increasing of hyper-parameter α. The decrease of performance is similar to traditional regularization with heavy or insufficient regularization.

And the best performance on the development is achieved in $\alpha = 0.6$ for *Zhuxian 600s*, $\alpha = 0.4$ for *Zhuxian 300s*. Note that a higher α makes the student network more focus on the target domain.

[2] *Patent 10*, *Patent 20* and *Patent 100* refer to the 10%, 20% and 100% of the Patent training data. *Zhuxian 300s* and *Zhuxian 600s* refer to the 300 and 600 sentences of the Zhuxian training data.

Methods	P	R	F1
(Li and Xue, 2016)			
Baseline	86.10	86.30	86.20
Patent 100	94.96	95.19	95.08
Ours			
Baseline	86.31	86.30	86.31
Mix *Patent 100*	94.56	94.39	94.47
Patent 100	95.13	95.26	95.20
+Patent 10	94.57	94.54	94.56
+Patent 20	94.95	95.09	95.02
+Patent 100	95.57	95.81	**95.69**

Table 4: The results between CTB7 and Patent. *Patent 10*, *Patent 20*, *Patent 100* refers to 10%, 20%, 100% of Patent train set. Mix refers to the method of training the model with mixed training data from Source and Target.

Methods	P	R	F1
(Zhang et al., 2014)			
Baseline	-	-	87.71
+Self-Training	-	-	88.62
+300	-	-	92.44
+300 +Self-Training	-	-	93.24
+3K +300	-	-	93.27
+3K +300 +Self-Training	-	-	93.98
+600	-	-	93.09
+600 +Self-Training	-	-	93.77
Ours			
Baseline	85.91	85.05	85.48
Mix 300	92.08	91.42	91.75
Mix 600	93.14	92.69	92.92
+300	93.61	93.30	93.45
+600	94.43	94.11	**94.27**

Table 5: The results between CTB5 and Zhuxian

The best development performance is achieved with different α is quite reasonable, because when the target domain data is becoming more and more sufficient, we can rely more on target domain data. And when the target domain data is sufficient to train a effective model by itself, we can use $\alpha = 1.0$ to turn off the regularization finally.

The similar results can also be found in the experiments between CTB7 to *Patent 10* and *Patent 20*. The best preformance of the student network is achieved when $\alpha = 0.5$ for *Patent 10*, $\alpha = 0.6$ for *Patent 20*.

3.4 Main Results

From CTB7 to Patent

We compare our neural regularized method with models from (Li and Xue, 2016) for the adaptation from CTB7 to Patent. The results are shown in Table 4. The performance of *Baseline* refers to the target domain performance of a baseline segmenter trained on source domain without any domain adaptation method. Li and Xue (2016) use a CRFs model as baseline model and improve the model from (Li and Xue, 2014). As shown in Table 4, the performance of our baseline model is comparable with their baseline model.

Li and Xue (Li and Xue, 2016) propose manually-crafted features to explore the domain-specific information in the patents and improve the accuracy of Chinese patent word segmentation. The manually-crafted features can be divided into *In-domain features* and *Out-of-domain features*. These features are used to model both the domain-specific characters combination and common cross-domain characteristics. They use the train set of Patent to train their model and the result is shown as *Patent 100*.

We employ the baseline model trained on the source domain as the teacher network and apply our neural regularized domain adaptation method to the student network with target domain data. Our method achieves a comparable performance with their model using only 20% of the Patent train set. We also list the performance of our method with 10%, 100% Patent train set as *+Patent 10* and *+Patent 100*. As the target domain data is often considered much 'expensive' comparing to publicly available source domain data, it is better to use as less target domain data as possible.

From CTB5 to Zhuxian

We also compare our methods with methods from (Zhang et al., 2014) for the adaptation from CTB5 to Zhuxian. The results are shown in Table 5. For (Zhang et al., 2014), manual annotated lexicon *3K*, self-training and two train set with 300/600 sentences are adopted. The annotated lexicon is used as plugins to the model for different domains through feature templates. The self-training method uses the model with lexicon features to label target domain sentences. Then the automatically labelled sentences are combined with source domain data to extend the training data. The annotated target domain sentences are directly mixed with source domain data as training data.

We train our teacher network with CTB5 training data and apply the teacher network to regularize the target domain specific training of the student network with our neural regularized domain adaptation method. Although Zhang et al. (2014) employ a joint model of word segmentation and POS tagging as baseline model, which is stronger than our single-task baseline model. Our neural regularized domain adaptation method still achieves a better result under the same target domain resources. It shows the effectiveness of our neural regularization method on exploring target domain information and preserving general knowledge.

3.5 Result Analysis

In this section, we show and analyse the results of different model on the target domain test data. We take the Patent as an example and pick three sentences from the test set of Patent as shown in Fig. 5. The *Baseline* in the figure refers to a baseline segmenter trained on source domain without any domain adaptation method. The *Patent20* in the figure refers to a baseline segmenter trained on target domain data *Patent 20* without any regularization from source domain. *Our method* refers to the model trained with our neural regularized domain adaptation method utilizing both the source domain teacher network and target domain data.

Take the third sentence as an example, the meaning of this sentence is "after the blank rod is sent,". This sentence contains both domain-specific words like "blank", "rod" and general words such as "after", "is sent". The *Baseline* is trained on source domain lacking the target domain-specific information, and therefore, makes mistakes when handling the domain-specific words. For example, the *Baseline* did not segment the "blank" and "rod" correctly in the third sentence.

The *Patent20* is trained on target domain data, but the training data is insufficient and leads to the lack of general knowledge. As shown in the figure, the *Patent20* segments the domain-specific words correctly while makes mistakes when facing the general words. The *Patent20* did not segment the general word "is sent" correctly.

Finally, with our neural regularized domain adaptation method, the neural model segments both domain-specific and general words correctly. It shows that our method explores the domain-specific information and preserves the general knowledge at the same time. The similar results can also be observed in other two sentences.

3.6 Experiments on the CTB9

We also perform our method between different genres of CTB9 as shown in Table 6. As mentioned in Sec. 3.1, in the CTB9, the source domain data is not significantly larger than target domain data. The nw, wb, sc, cs refer to *Newswire*, *Weblogs*, *SMS/Chat messages*, *conversational speech* respectively. The nw is chosen as the source domain data and the others are employed as the target domain data.

nw − > wb			
Methods	P	R	F1
Baseline	86.45	88.04	87.24
Target only	90.90	89.67	90.28
Mix	92.64	92.41	92.52
Our method	92.91	92.40	**92.65**
nw − > sc			
Methods	P	R	F1
Baseline	80.49	80.98	80.74
Target only	94.93	94.21	94.57
Mix	94.93	94.66	94.80
Our method	94.92	94.91	**94.92**
nw − > cs			
Methods	P	R	F1
Baseline	82.86	82.21	82.53
Target only	95.94	95.64	95.79
Mix	96.10	96.02	96.06
Our method	96.32	96.68	**96.50**

Table 6: The experiment results of CTB9 between nw and wb, sc, cs genres.

The *Baseline* refers to the target domain performance of a baseline segmenter trained with the *Newswire* data. The *Target only* refers to the target domain performance of a baseline segmenter trained with the target domain data only. The *Our method* refers to the performance of our neural regularized domain adaptation method.

Because few previous methods are adopted in CTB9, we only compare our method with a baseline model trained on source domain and a baseline model trained on target domain providing the performance of our method for further comparision of domain adaptation methods in the future. Our method achieves improvement over both *Baseline* and *Target only*.

4 Related Work

Domain adaptation can be roughly divided into the fully-supervised and the semi-supervised domain adaptation (Daume III, 2007). Much work has been done in this area. For example, in the fully-supervised scenario, the well-known method *Easy Adaptation* is proposed to augment the feature space of both source and target data and then the combined feature space is used to train cross-domain model(Daume III, 2007). Daumé III et al. (2010) then proposed a semi-supervised extension

Baseline: 载有 喷 过 砂 的 连杆 的 专用 托盘， ×
Patent20: 载有 喷过砂 的 连杆 的 专用 托盘， ×
Our method: 载有 喷过 砂 的 连杆 的 专用 托盘， √
contains sprayed sand rod special tray

Baseline: 取下 连 杆盖 9 并 对 破开 部位 进行 清洁， ×
Patent20: 取下 连杆 盖 9 并 对 破开 部位 进行 清洁， ×
Our method: 取下 连杆盖 9 并 对 破开 部位 进行 清洁， √
remove the cap of rod 9 and to broken part do clean

Baseline: 在 毛坯连杆 送到 后， ×
Patent20: 在 毛坯 连杆 送 到 后， ×
Our method: 在 毛坯 连杆 送到 后， √
after blank rod is sent

Figure 5: The results of different model on the same three test sentences of the Patent.

of the *Easy Adaptation*, which harnesses unlabeled target domain data to ameliorate the transfer of information from source to target.

Knowledge Distillation is first proposed to compress the knowledge of a source model (Bucilu et al., 2006) into a smaller target model. Hinton et al. (2015) developed this approach using a different compression technique. (Lopez-Paz et al., 2015) proposed a framework unifying *Knowledge Distillation* (Hinton et al., 2015) and *privileged information* (Vapnik and Izmailov, 2015). As *Knowledge Distillation* is able to transfer knowledge, it has been extended to other tasks. Li and Hoiem (2016) adopted a method to gradually add new capabilities to a multi-task system while preserve the original capabilities. Hu et al. (2016) employed *Knowledge Distillation* to enhance various types of neural networks with declarative first-order logic rules. Ao et al. (2017) utilized the unlabeled data to transfer the knowledge from the source models and SVM was used as base classifier to efficiently solve the imitation parameter.

For Chinese word segmentation, previous works mainly focused on semi-supervised domain adaptation methods. Unsupervised character clustering feature and self-training method were explored (Liu and Zhang, 2012). The partially-annotated data was found to be more effective than lexicons based features (Liu et al., 2014). The effectiveness of manually annotated lexicons and sentences were explored and compared (Zhang et al., 2014). Li and Xue (2014) designed *In-domain* and *Out-of-domain* features to capture the distributional characteristics in patents and annotated a significant amount of Chinese patent data (Li and Xue, 2016). Qiu and Zhang (2015) reduced the burden of the manually annotated lexicons by mining entities in Chinese novel with information extraction techniques.

5 Conclusion

In this paper, we focus on the fully-supervised domain adaptation for Chinese word segmentation and propose a neural regularized domain adaptation method. As the amount of annotated data in target domain is limited, it is insufficient to directly train a effective model and avoid overfitting. In our method, teacher networks trained in source domain are employed as general background knowledge to regularize the training process of the student network.

We investigate that the effect of hyper-parameter α is similar to the hyper-parameter of traditional weights regularization. Then we evaluate our method in the adaptation of two target domain datasets, from CTB5 to Zhuxian and from CTB7 to Patent. Experiments show that our neural regularized domain adaptation method can achieve improved performance with previous domain adaptation methods. We also analyse the results and display some examples, which shows that our method explores the domain-specific information and preserves the general knowledge at the same time. Finally, we apply our method to different genres of CTB9 and provide the results for further comparision in the future.

Acknowledge

This work was supported by Beijing Natural Science Foundation (4174098), National Natural Science Foundation of China (61702047) and the Fundamental Research Funds for the Central Universities (2017RC02).

References

Shuang Ao, Xiang Li, and Charles X Ling. 2017. Fast generalized distillation for semi-supervised domain adaptation. In *AAAI*. pages 1719–1725.

John Blitzer, Mark Dredze, Fernando Pereira, et al. 2007. Biographies, bollywood, boom-boxes and blenders: Domain adaptation for sentiment classification. In *ACL*. volume 7, pages 440–447.

Cristian Bucilu, Rich Caruana, and Alexandru Niculescu-Mizil. 2006. Model compression. In *Proceedings of the 12th ACM SIGKDD international conference on Knowledge discovery and data mining*. ACM, pages 535–541.

Xinchi Chen, Xipeng Qiu, and Xuanjing Huang. 2016. A long dependency aware deep architecture for joint chinese word segmentation and pos tagging. *arXiv preprint arXiv:1611.05384* .

Xinchi Chen, Zhan Shi, Xipeng Qiu, and Xuanjing Huang. 2017. Adversarial multi-criteria learning for chinese word segmentation. *arXiv preprint arXiv:1704.07556* http://arxiv.org/abs/1704.07556.

Ronan Collobert, Jason Weston, Léon Bottou, Michael Karlen, Koray Kavukcuoglu, and Pavel Kuksa. 2011. Natural language processing (almost) from scratch. *The Journal of Machine Learning Research* 12:2493–2537.

Hal Daume III. 2007. Frustratingly easy domain adaptation. In *Proceedings of the 45th Annual Meeting of the Association of Computational Linguistics*. Association for Computational Linguistics, pages 256–263. http://aclweb.org/anthology/P07-1033.

Hal Daumé III, Abhishek Kumar, and Avishek Saha. 2010. Frustratingly easy semi-supervised domain adaptation. In *Proceedings of the 2010 Workshop on Domain Adaptation for Natural Language Processing*. Association for Computational Linguistics, pages 53–59.

Thomas Emerson. 2005. The second international chinese word segmentation bakeoff. In *Proceedings of the Fourth SIGHAN Workshop on Chinese Language Processing*. http://aclweb.org/anthology/I05-3017.

Yaroslav Ganin, Evgeniya Ustinova, Hana Ajakan, Pascal Germain, Hugo Larochelle, François Laviolette, Mario Marchand, and Victor Lempitsky. 2016. Domain-adversarial training of neural networks. *Journal of Machine Learning Research* 17(59):1–35.

Jun Hatori, Takuya Matsuzaki, Yusuke Miyao, and Jun'ichi Tsujii. 2012. Incremental joint approach to word segmentation, pos tagging, and dependency parsing in chinese. In *Proceedings of the 50th Annual Meeting of the Association for Computational Linguistics (Volume 1: Long Papers)*. Association for Computational Linguistics, pages 1045–1053. http://aclweb.org/anthology/P12-1110.

Geoffrey Hinton, Oriol Vinyals, and Jeff Dean. 2015. Distilling the knowledge in a neural network. *arXiv preprint arXiv:1503.02531* .

Zhiting Hu, Xuezhe Ma, Zhengzhong Liu, Eduard Hovy, and Eric Xing. 2016. Harnessing deep neural networks with logic rules. *arXiv preprint arXiv:1603.06318* .

Wenbin Jiang, Liang Huang, and Qun Liu. 2009. Automatic adaptation of annotation standards: Chinese word segmentation and pos tagging – a case study. In *Proceedings of the Joint Conference of the 47th Annual Meeting of the ACL and the 4th International Joint Conference on Natural Language Processing of the AFNLP*. Association for Computational Linguistics, pages 522–530. http://aclweb.org/anthology/P09-1059.

Jin Kiat Low, Hwee Tou Ng, and Wenyuan Guo. 2005. A maximum entropy approach to chinese word segmentation. In *Proceedings of the Fourth SIGHAN Workshop on Chinese Language Processing*. http://aclweb.org/anthology/I05-3025.

Yoon Kim. 2014. Convolutional neural networks for sentence classification. In *Proceedings of the 2014 Conference on Empirical Methods in Natural Language Processing (EMNLP)*. Association for Computational Linguistics, pages 1746–1751.

Si Li and Nianwen Xue. 2014. Effective document-level features for chinese patent word segmentation. In *Proceedings of the 52nd Annual Meeting of the Association for Computational Linguistics (Volume 2: Short Papers)*. Association for Computational Linguistics, pages 199–205. https://doi.org/10.3115/v1/P14-2033.

Si Li and Nianwen Xue. 2016. Towards accurate word segmentation for chinese patents. *arXiv preprint arXiv:1611.10038* .

Zhizhong Li and Derek Hoiem. 2016. Learning without forgetting. In *European Conference on Computer Vision*. Springer, pages 614–629.

Yang Liu and Yue Zhang. 2012. Unsupervised domain adaptation for joint segmentation and pos-tagging. In *Proceedings of COLING 2012: Posters*. The COLING 2012 Organizing Committee, pages 745–754. http://aclweb.org/anthology/C12-2073.

Yijia Liu, Yue Zhang, Wanxiang Che, Ting Liu, and Fan Wu. 2014. Domain adaptation for crf-based chinese word segmentation using free annotations. In *Proceedings of the 2014 Conference on Empirical Methods in Natural Language Processing (EMNLP)*. Association for Computational Linguistics, pages 864–874. https://doi.org/10.3115/v1/D14-1093.

David Lopez-Paz, Léon Bottou, Bernhard Schölkopf, and Vladimir Vapnik. 2015. Unifying distillation and privileged information. *arXiv preprint arXiv:1511.03643* .

Fuchun Peng, Fangfang Feng, and Andrew McCallum. 2004. Chinese segmentation and new word detection using conditional random fields. In *COLING 2004: Proceedings of the 20th International Conference on Computational Linguistics*. http://aclweb.org/anthology/C04-1081.

Likun Qiu and Yue Zhang. 2015. Word segmentation for chinese novels. In *AAAI*. pages 2440–2446.

Artem Rozantsev, Mathieu Salzmann, and Pascal Fua. 2016. Beyond sharing weights for deep domain adaptation. *arXiv preprint arXiv:1603.06432* .

Sebastian Ruder, Parsa Ghaffari, and John G Breslin. 2017. Knowledge adaptation: Teaching to adapt. *arXiv preprint arXiv:1702.02052* .

Weiwei Sun. 2011. A stacked sub-word model for joint chinese word segmentation and part-of-speech tagging. In *Proceedings of the 49th Annual Meeting of the Association for Computational Linguistics: Human Language Technologies*. Association for Computational Linguistics, pages 1385–1394. http://aclweb.org/anthology/P11-1139.

Vladimir Vapnik and Rauf Izmailov. 2015. Learning using privileged information: similarity control and knowledge transfer. *Journal of Machine Learning Research* 16:2023–2049.

Naiwen Xue, Fei Xia, Fu-Dong Chiou, and Marta Palmer. 2005. The penn chinese treebank: Phrase structure annotation of a large corpus. *Natural language engineering* 11(02):207–238.

Nianwen Xue. 2003. Chinese word segmentation as character tagging. In *International Journal of Computational Linguistics & Chinese Language Processing, Volume 8, Number 1, February 2003: Special Issue on Word Formation and Chinese Language Processing*. pages 29–48. http://aclweb.org/anthology/O03-4002.

Dong Yu, Kaisheng Yao, Hang Su, Gang Li, and Frank Seide. 2013. Kl-divergence regularized deep neural network adaptation for improved large vocabulary speech recognition. In *IEEE International Conference on Acoustics, Speech and Signal Processing*. pages 7893–7897.

Matthew D Zeiler. 2012. Adadelta: an adaptive learning rate method. *arXiv preprint arXiv:1212.5701* .

Meishan Zhang, Yue Zhang, Wanxiang Che, and Ting Liu. 2014. Type-supervised domain adaptation for joint segmentation and pos-tagging. In *Proceedings of the 14th Conference of the European Chapter of the Association for Computational Linguistics*. Association for Computational Linguistics, pages 588–597. https://doi.org/10.3115/v1/E14-1062.

Meishan Zhang, Yue Zhang, and Guohong Fu. 2016. Transition-based neural word segmentation. In *Proceedings of the 54th Annual Meeting of the Association for Computational Linguistics (Volume 1: Long Papers)*. Association for Computational Linguistics, pages 421–431. https://doi.org/10.18653/v1/P16-1040.

Yue Zhang and Stephen Clark. 2008. Joint word segmentation and pos tagging using a single perceptron. In *Proceedings of ACL-08: HLT*. Association for Computational Linguistics, pages 888–896. http://aclweb.org/anthology/P08-1101.

The Sentimental Value of Chinese Sub-Character Components

Yassine Benajiba **Or Biran** **Zhiliang Weng** **Yong Zhang** **Jin Sun**

Mainiway AI Lab

{yassine,or.biran,zhiliang.weng,yong.zhang,jin.sun}@mainiway.com

Abstract

Sub-character components of Chinese characters carry important semantic information, and recent studies have shown that utilizing this information can improve performance on core semantic tasks. In this paper, we hypothesize that in addition to semantic information, sub-character components may also carry emotional information, and that utilizing it should improve performance on sentiment analysis tasks. We conduct a series of experiments on four Chinese sentiment data sets and show that we can significantly improve the performance in various tasks over that of a character-level embeddings baseline. We then focus on qualitatively assessing multiple examples and trying to explain how the sub-character components affect the results in each case.

1 Introduction

Chinese characters are composed of one or more *components*, which may have a phonetic or semantic meaning. A special type of component is a *radical*, which is the component under which a character is traditionally listed in the dictionary. Radicals, in particular, often carry a semantic meaning. For example, the character 媽 (*mā*, "mother") is composed of the semantic component, which is also the radical, 女 (*nǔ*, "female") and the phonetic component 馬 (*mǎ*, "horse").

Recently, there has been growing focus on utilizing sub-character components, such as radicals, in natural language processing. These components can carry intrinsic semantic information that complements the contextual information that is utilized, e.g., in building word embeddings. It has been shown that embeddings which are constructed with a combination of radical, character and word level granulairty outperform those that lack the radical information on classical semantic tasks such as analogy and paraphrasing (Sun et al., 2014; Li et al., 2015; Yin et al., 2016; Yu et al., 2017).

In this paper, we explore the hypothesis that in addition to the sort of hard semantic tasks that they have so far been applied to, sub-character components can also carry *sentiment*-related or *emotional* information, and therefore should be useful in sentiment analysis as well. In particular, we have in mind three types of sentiment-related information in semantic components:

1. Components that have a specific polarity, such as 疒 ("disease") which is generally found in negative characters, or 子 ("child") which is somewhat more common in positive characters

2. Components that do not specify a polarity, but specify subjectivity or emotional content, such as 心 ("heart") or 忄 ("heart" in vertical form)

3. Components that are objective, but because of human tendencies are more likely to appear in characters that tend to appear in subjective context and may tend towards a particular polarity or intensity, such as 虫 ("insect") or 贝 ("treasure")

To test our hypothesis, we conduct experiments on multiple Chinese datasets annotated for sentiment or emotion, both at the

Proceedings of the 9th SIGHAN Workshop on Chinese Language Processing, pages 21–29,
Taipei, Taiwan, December 1, 2017. ©2017 AFNLP

word level and the phrase level, and show that using various forms of sub-character information significantly helps with correctly determining the sentiment of the text, and that combining them achieves the best results.

2 Related Work

Work on sentiment analysis started in the mid 1990's (Wiebe and Bruce, 1995; Hatzivassiloglou and McKeown, 1997), and initially relied heavily on lexicon-based methods and applied mostly to newswire data. Later on, statistical and distributional methods (Pang and Lee, 2005; Wilson et al., 2005; Socher et al., 2011) became prevalent, most recently with Deep Neural Nets (Tang et al., 2015; Poria et al., 2015; Qian et al., 2017). The domain of interest has also shifted, from newswire to social media, in particular blogs (Mei et al., 2007; Yu and Kübler, 2011) and microblogs (Go et al., 2009; Agarwal et al., 2011; Kiritchenko et al., 2014).

Although the availability of sentiment annotated Chinese corpora is limited, Chinese language sentiment analysis has also become an active research area in recent years. Most work in this area fits into three broad categories. One approach relies on bilingual knowledge to first translate the Chinese text into English text, and then leverage the abundance of English resources for sentiment analysis (Wan, 2008). The second focuses on lexical-based or rule-based sentiment scoring. For example, Xianghua et al. (2013) classify the polarity of the text using the HowNet lexicon, while Zhang et al. (2009) use word dependency rules to determine the sentiment of a sentence. The third approach employs supervised learning on a manually tagged dataset using specialized features (Tan and Zhang, 2008) or on automatically labeled data, e.g. Chinese tweets containing unambiguous emoticons (Zhao et al., 2012). Shared tasks relevant to Chinese sentiment analysis have become prevalent in recent years, and include the SIGHAN 2015 task on Topic-Based Chinese Message Polarity Classification (Liao et al., 2015), the IALP 2016 task on Dimensional Sentiment Analysis for Chinese Words (Yu et al., 2016b), and the upcoming IJCNLP 2017 task on Dimensional Sentiment Analysis for Chinese Phrases.

Work utilizing radicals and other sub-character components is fairly uncommon. One line of research which has become increasingly popular is focused on augmenting word- and character-level embeddings with sub-character information. Sun et al. (2014) and Li et al. (2015) used radicals to enhance the C&W model (Collobert and Weston, 2008) and the word2vec model (Mikolov et al., 2013), respectively. Yin et al. (2016) and later Yu et al. (2017) had shown that word embeddings of the CWE variety (Chen et al., 2015) created from a combination of word-level, character-level, and sub-character-level information outperformed those coming from a single granularity level on semantic tasks. Yu et al. (2017), in particular, show that in addition to radicals, other sub-character components are useful as well.

Ke and Hagiwara (2017) used embeddings created from the radicals of characters and used them in sentiment classification. They showed that their model performs as well on this task with these embeddings as with character-level embeddings, which require a higher-dimensional model and many more parameters. This is the only work, to our knowledge, which uses sub-character components for a sentiment task. Their work differs from ours in several ways, the most important being that they aim to use the radical-level embeddings *instead* of the character-level ones, showing that they can replicate the performance with fewer parameters; in contrast, our work investigates whether or not sub-character components contain useful sentiment information *beyond* that of contextual embeddings, and shows that they complement one another. In addition, we explore the use of non-radical components, in addition to radicals.

The only work, to our knowledge, which makes use not of a list of components but of the order of strokes (Bishun), which are the atomic units of Chinese characters, is by Mi et al. (2016) who used the stroke order predict the correct pronounciation of a character.

3 Approach

Since we are interested mostly in showing the value of the sub-character information, our focus is on performing experiments with various tasks, data sets and representations, and less on the model used in classification. We therefore perform all experiments with a single, straightforward Neural Network (NN) architecture, described below. In addition to using the radicals from a provided list, we devised a second representation of sub-character components, derived directly from the stroke order of the character.

3.1 Character level Embedding

Word embeddings have been very popular in recent years because of the significant improvement they brought about in almost all the subfields of NLP. Across these subfields, this meant not only a good way of dealing with the dimensionality problem, which is often encountered with one-hot encoding, but also a completely unsupervised, i.e. cheap, solution to create semantic spaces that encode most of the relationships among words in the vocabulary of a language.

The idea of encoding each word as a D-dimensional vector is not new (Levy et al., 2015); however, since the publication of the *word2vec* (Mikolov et al., 2013) paper we finally have a method that encompasses the algorithm together with the right negative sampling approach and hyper-parameters. In the paper, the authors explain that in order to compute the vectors representing the words w_i of a certain vocabulary V (of dimension $|V|$), it suffices to use a one hidden layer NN that tries to predict the current word given the neighboring words (CBOW) or the other way around (Skip-Gram).

The optimization function that aims at maximizing the probability between a word w and a context c is thus expressed as follows:

$$p(w|c) = \frac{e^s(w,c)}{\sum_{i=1}^{|V|} e^s(w_i,c)} \qquad (1)$$

By making the hidden layer of a much lower dimensionality than $|V|$ we end up with word representations that are much lighter (we can now represent each word with only D dimensions) and bear semantic value (words that appear in similar contexts have vectors that are closer to each other in the semantic space).

In the work we present in this paper, we wanted to use Chinese word embeddings instead of a one-hot representation to take advantage of these properties. However, since our goal was also to investigate an approach that does not rely on heavy preprocessing (such as word segmentation) and that could work equally well on words, phrases and sentences, we found it challenging to use *word2vec*. A more convenient approach, which we employ here, is *fastText* (Bojanowski et al., 2017). This approach relies on the same intuition as *word2vec*, but has the advantage that it builds embeddings for the character n-grams that compose a word. By taking morphology into consideration, *fastText* is able to build embeddings for unseen words (including words with typos) which *word2vec* cannot. From a Chinese morphology perspective, however, this allows to build embeddings for a word, phrase or sentences using its constituent characters without the need of any preprocessing. In a sense, this is similar to computing the vector representing a sentence as the average of the *word2vec* vectors of its constituent words. Despite the simplicity of this approach and its undermining of syntax, it has proved to work very well in combination with deep dense networks yielding results that surpass those obtained with LSTMs (Iyyer et al., 2015). Our choice of learning model, which we describe in Section 3.2, is based on this idea.

3.2 Our Learning Machine

As we previously mentioned, Deep Averaging Networks (DANs) (Iyyer et al., 2015) is one of the most successful approaches to classifying embedded representations. As the authors describe in the paper, the results show that through applying N layers of non-linearity, the network is capable of boosting/shrinking the values of the dimensions that most/least contribute to the classification task. In their work, the authors have a first layer that computes the pointwise average embedding of the words in a sentence as follows:

$$av = \frac{\sum_{i=1}^{W} w_i}{W} \qquad (2)$$

In our architecture, this layer is removed and the averaging operation is delegated to *fastText* as we want it to be performed at

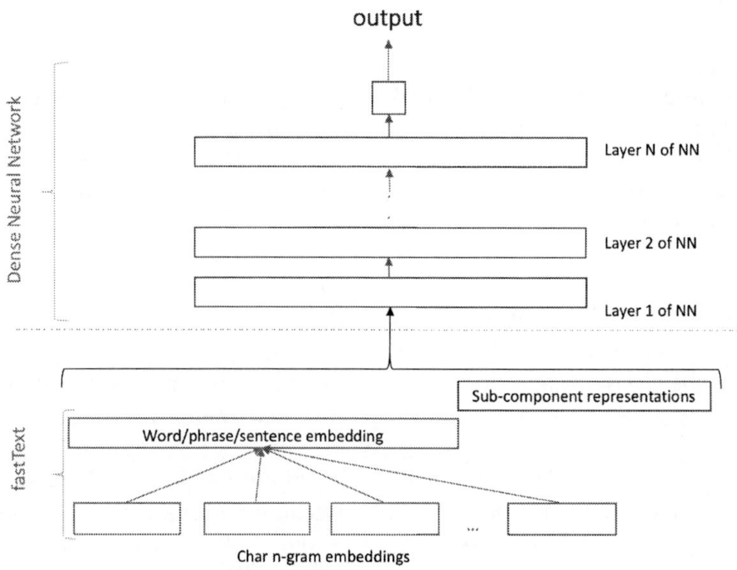

Figure 1: Architecture of a dense NN using fastText embeddings as an input. Output is a one dimension layer in case of regression and softmax for classification.

the character n-gram level. The sub component representations are subsequently concatenated (see Figure 1).

At each hidden layer h_i we apply a non-linear function to its input that can be described as:

$$h_i = f(W_i + b_i) \quad (3)$$

Where W_i and b_i are the parameters of the hidden layer. When performing classification, we apply the softmax function to the last layer. The softmax function ensures that our output is a probability distribution over our set of classes.

We experiment with one and three hidden layers and report the results accordingly. We keep the optimization function (adam) and the activation function (ReLU) fixed in all of the reported results. The dimensionality of the embeddings is 300.

3.3 Sub-Component Representations

We use the code made available by Yu et al. (2017) to collect the list of the components (one of which is the radical) for 20,879 characters. In our experiments, we use a one-hot representation for the 214 radicals and concatenate this representation with *fastText* embeddings (Bojanowski et al., 2017).

In addition, we employ a bottom-up approach using the stroke order for each character[1]. From this data, we collect all stroke n-grams for $n = 1 \ldots 7$ and sort them by frequency. In our experiments, we use a one-hot representation of the k most frequent n-grams (trying a range of values for k) and concatenate these with the *fastText* embeddings. Unlike the radicals representation above, this approach has the potential of using non-radical sub-character information, and even information coming from combinations of components; it also has the advantage that it comes directly from the order of strokes, of which there are just over 20 types, instead of representing each component as a unique unit.

4 Data Sets

In order to investigate the usefulness of our approach on a variety of tasks, domains and text characteristics (e.g., length and style) we perform experiments on four datasets.

The first data set is the widely used **NTUSD** (Ku and Chen, 2007) - a sentiment dictionary containing binary polarity an-

[1]We scraped the stroke order for 25,723 Chinese characters from `https://bihua.51240.com/`

Data set	Total size	Entry length	# of labels	# of categories
NTUSD	11,088	Single word	1	2
CVAW	3,552	Single word	2	Continuous
CVAP	3,000	Short phrase	2	Continuous
Weibo	333,044	Microblog entry	1	4

Table 1: The four data sets and their properties.

notations (positive/negative) for over 11,000 words.

The next two data sets come from this year's IJCNLP shared task on Dimensional Sentiment Analysis for Chinese Phrases (DSAP). In this task, terms are labeled with two numeric values, one for the *valence* of the term and one for the *arousal*, together comprising the term's location in the valence-arousal affect space (Russell, 1980). The task is evaluated on two data sets: **CVAW**, which contains 2,802 and 750 annotated single words in its training and test set, respectively (Yu et al., 2016a); and **CVAP**, which similarly contains 2,250 and 750 short phrases.

Finally, we include the **Weibo** emotion data set, collected by Fan et al. (2014) from Weibo, a Chinese microblogging service, and automatically annotated with emotional content. The data set contains over 333,000 entries, each labeled with one of four emotions: joy, anger, sadness or disgust. In comparison with the words of NTUSD and CVAW, and even the short phrases of CVAP, the Weibo entries are significantly longer (the longest entries contain over 400 characters) and like most social media, exhibit unusual linguistic style.

In the cases of NTUSD and Weibo, since there is no pre-determined separation into training and test sets, we randomized the data and set apart 10% of the instances as a test set.

Table 1 summarizes the differences between the four data sets.

5 Experiments

We conduct experiments on all four data sets with the following representation combinations. The baseline is the fastText embeddings, without any sub-character information; we then try the embeddings plus our radicals representation, and the embeddings plus the top k n-grams representation for $k \in \{100, 250, 500, 700\}$. Finally, we use the embeddings, radicals, and n-gram representation together.

For each combination, we try both a single-layer NN and a 3-layer NN, to see whether or not depth has a significant impact on the results.

Note that because of the different tasks (and label types), the four data sets require different evaluation metrics. In particular, CVAW and CVAP are evaluated using the mean absolute error (MAE) and the Pearson correlation coefficient (PCC) for valence and arousal separately, while NTUSD and Weibo are evaluated with Micro-F1.

5.1 Results

The results for the single-layer architecture are shown in Table 2, and the results for the three-layer architecture in Table 3.

Across the board, adding the sub-components representations to the *fastText* embeddings always outperforms the approach that resorts only to the latter. The only exception observed is when we predict valence for phrases, i.e. CVAP1, in a three layer NN.

For valence, adding sub-component representations reduced the MAE by up to 0.07 points (from 0.91 to 0.839) in a one layer NN, and 0.03 points when using a three layer network; whereas for arousal, the MAE was reduced by 0.18 in (from 1.12 to 0.94) in the one layer NN and 0.104 in a three layer NN. PCC was also improved accordingly.

Similarly, for the NTUSD data set, we obtained an improvement of 3.4 f-score points in the one layer NN (from 61.2 to 64.6) and 0.4 points in a three layer NN.

When classifying long sentences, i.e. Weibo data, we obtained an improvement of 2 points of f-measure in the one-layer NN and up to 6 (0.54 vs 0.60) points of improvements in the 3 layer NN. This result is interesting because it shows how the sub component representa-

Combination	NTUSD	Weibo	CVAW				CVAP			
			Valence		Arousal		Valence		Arousal	
	F1	F1	MAE	PCC	MAE	PCC	MAE	PCC	MAE	PCC
FastText	61.2	59.2	0.91	0.694	1.125	0.436	0.827	0.781	0.658	0.727
FT+radicals	63.5	60.1	0.882	0.71	1.024	0.488	0.803	0.78	0.609	0.755
FT+ngrams(100)	63.4	59.1	0.855	0.724	1.055	0.479	0.832	0.765	0.603	0.756
FT+ngrams(250)	61.9	56.6	0.871	0.735	1.0	0.523	0.861	0.737	0.576	0.758
FT+ngrams(500)	62.6	57.4	0.896	0.726	0.979	0.52	0.825	0.755	0.586	0.758
FT+ngrams(700)	**64.6**	56.7	0.907	0.728	0.949	0.532	0.813	0.755	0.589	0.754
FT+rad.+ng(100)	62.1	60.8	**0.839**	**0.739**	0.982	0.554	0.793	0.764	0.677	0.766
FT+rad.+ng(250)	62.2	59.7	0.861	0.74	0.966	0.557	0.794	0.772	**0.567**	**0.772**
FT+rad.+ng(500)	57.8	**61.6**	0.867	0.742	0.969	0.533	**0.777**	**0.772**	0.586	0.773
FT+rad.+ng(700)	64.3	60.1	0.859	0.739	**0.945**	**0.553**	0.787	0.763	1.869	0.708

Table 2: The experimental results with one layer.

Combination	NTUSD	Weibo	CVAW				CVAP			
			Valence		Arousal		Valence		Arousal	
	F1	F1	MAE	PCC	MAE	PCC	MAE	PCC	MAE	PCC
FastText	63.7	54.1	0.827	0.738	1.029	0.497	**0.652**	**0.847**	0.587	0.765
FT+radicals	62.3	59.3	0.81	0.756	0.975	0.518	0.69	0.821	0.559	0.786
FT+ngrams(100)	63.6	58.3	0.824	0.752	0.972	0.534	0.71	0.803	0.596	0.758
FT+ngrams(250)	62.7	59.9	0.834	0.754	0.953	0.547	0.742	0.79	0.639	0.722
FT+ngrams(500)	61.8	**60.8**	0.798	0.762	0.94	0.549	0.719	0.795	**0.551**	**0.776**
FT+ngrams(700)	63.6	57.2	0.838	0.753	0.93	0.556	0.772	0.773	0.572	0.767
FT+rad.+ng(100)	61.4	60.2	**0.796**	**0.764**	0.948	0.557	0.706	0.821	0.568	0.773
FT+rad.+ng(250)	63.6	60.1	0.809	0.763	0.939	0.554	0.698	0.807	0.624	0.741
FT+rad.+ng(500)	**64.1**	55.7	0.799	0.756	**0.925**	**0.574**	0.769	0.765	0.588	0.757
FT+rad.+ng(700)	63.5	55.5	0.833	0.765	0.948	0.556	0.777	0.766	1.341	0.347

Table 3: The experimental results with three layers.

tions can help maintain a high performance even when the text is long. Using *fastText* only, however, yields poor results even if we increase the number of hidden layers.

Overall, the sub-component representations consistently improve results although the improvement is bigger for shallower networks.

5.2 Analysis

In this section, we go through a number of examples where the sub-character features were helpful and a few where they introduced errors. In all cases, we try to explain why the difference might have emerged.

In NTUSD, there are many cases where one or both of the variants made the correct prediction while the embeddings-only baseline did not. For example, the baseline predicts that 好学 ("studious") is negative, which is wrong; the two radicals, 女 ("woman") and 子 ("child") are both somewhat more likely to appear in positive characters, which in this case pushes the classifier in the right direction. Other words which are classified correctly by all of our variants, but not the baseline, include 严酷的 ("cruel") and 勇敢的 ("brave").

In the case of 败俗 ("ruined"), the baseline as well as the radicals representation made an error. The ngrams representation, however, got it right. We believe this is because of the radical 贝 ("treasure"), which usually appears in positive characters. In this case, the ngram representation has multiple variants of this radical and some subsequent strokes, which may explain how it can more accurately separate between sets of characters. Other cases like this include 狼心狗肺 ("ungrateful and cold-blooded") and 法西斯党员 ("fascist party members"). In contrast, in the case of 犯过错 ("made a mistake"), the radicals representation made the correct prediction, possibly because of the radical 犭 ("dog"), which despite seeming objective often appears in characters having to do with animals or animal characteristics, which in Chinese tend to appear in negative contexts. The baseline made an incorrect prediction here, and so did the n-gram variants, for reasons that are not entirely clear to us. In general, we expect the ngram representations to be wrong more often for words with rare radicals that may not make the threshold, or with radicals that are composed of many strokes and cannot be represented well by 7-grams.

In some cases, the baseline gets it right while all of our variants fail. In some of these cases, it is not immediately intuitive that these really are subjective words: 命运注定的 ("predestined") and 有贵族气派的 ("aristocratic"), for example. This semantic ambiguity may make it a task more suitable for embeddings, and the sub-character components could simply be adding noise. Another example where our variants fail is 雄辩 ("eloquent"); in this case, we have two fairly rare radicals - 隹 ("short-tailed bird") and 辛 ("bitter"), which we likely have sparse data for. In addition, the second radical is more often seen in negative characters, which may in this case push the classifier in the wrong direction.

In CVAW, instead of binary labels, we have continuous dimensions which provides a more granular view. One interesting example from this data set is 异常死亡 ("abnormal death"), which has a valence of 1.42, very negative. With embeddings alone, the classifier ends up with a very bad prediction: 6.38 - far into the positive side. This is likely because the first two characters of 异常死亡 are not negative, while the last two (both having to do with death) appear in a diverse context which is not always (perhaps not often) negative. The radical 歹 ("death") of the third word, however, is a clearly negative radical which pushes our variants towards the negative end, arriving at a prediction of 4.97 - still not great, but on the negative side of valence. Similar examples include 极为优秀 ("very good") and 本来有点同情 ("originally a bit sympathetic").

The sub-character components add much more to arousal prediction, however. It may be because arousal is less likely to be modeled well in embeddings (since the context for similar words with different arousal levels can be very similar), while some radicals model it directly. The word 极为震怒 ("extremely angry") has a gold arousal value of 8.56, very high. the embeddings alone predict 4.21, which is far from it and on the low arousal side. With radicals, we arrive at 5.46, much closer and on the high arousal side. This is likely because of two radicals associated with higher arousal, on average: 心 ("heart") and 雨 ("rain"). The stroke ngrams, in this case, do better than the baseline but not as well as the radicals: 4.91. In other cases, such as 很担心 ("very worried"), the ngrams perform significantly higher than the radicals.

Although interesting, examples from the longer texts in CVAP and Weibo are very difficult to analyze. We leave it to future work to explore these data sets beyond our quantitative evaluation.

6 Conclusion

We showed through experiments on multiple data sets that sub-character components, represented either as a set of radicals or as stroke n-grams, contain information that is useful in sentiment classification beyond the semantic information encoded in character-level embeddings. We showed that with a few exceptions, this effect can be seen with a variety of text lengths and linguistic styles, as well as with varying model depths.

One problem that is inherent to both the *word2vec* and *fastText* approaches is that the embeddings of negative and positive sentiment words, e.g. *good* and *bad*, tend to be very similar because they occur in similar contexts; similar behavior exists for emotional dimensions other than polarity (e.g., arousal). In ideographic languages such as Chinese, we can leverage the fact that the characters themselves contain sentiment cues which cannot easily be found with a distributional approach.

We illustrated with specific examples the advantages and disadvantages of the two representations, and showed experimentally that they are in fact complementary, and we can generally achieve the best performance by using both. We also show that using sub-character components yield much more improvement when dealing with long text. We leave the exploration of additional useful representations, as well as the best model to use them with, to future work.

References

Apoorv Agarwal, Boyi Xie, Ilia Vovsha, Owen Rambow, and Rebecca Passonneau. 2011. Sentiment analysis of twitter data. In *Proceedings of the Workshop on Languages in Social Media*. LSM '11, pages 30–38.

Piotr Bojanowski, Edouard Grave, Armand Joulin, and Tomas Mikolov. 2017. Enriching word vectors with subword information. *Transactions of the Association for Computational Linguistics* 5:135–146.

Xinxiong Chen, Lei Xu, Zhiyuan Liu, Maosong Sun, and Huan-Bo Luan. 2015. Joint learning of character and word embeddings. In *IJCAI*. pages 1236–1242.

Ronan Collobert and Jason Weston. 2008. A unified architecture for natural language processing: Deep neural networks with multitask learning. In *Proceedings of the 25th International Conference on Machine Learning*. ICML '08, pages 160–167.

Rui Fan, Jichang Zhao, Yan Chen, and Ke Xu. 2014. Anger is more influential than joy: Sentiment correlation in weibo. *PloS one* 9(10):e110184.

Alec Go, Richa Bhayani, and Lei Huang. 2009. Twitter sentiment classification using distant supervision. *CS224N Project Report, Stanford* 1(2009):12.

Vasileios Hatzivassiloglou and Kathleen McKeown. 1997. Predicting the semantic orientation of adjectives. In *Proceedings of the Joint ACL/EACL Conference*. pages 174–181.

M. Iyyer, V. Manjunatha, J. Boyd-Graber, and H Daume III. 2015. Deep unordered composition rivals syntactic methods for text classification. In *ACL*. pages 1681–1689.

Y. Ke and M. Hagiwara. 2017. Radical-level Ideograph Encoder for RNN-based Sentiment Analysis of Chinese and Japanese. *ArXiv e-prints* .

Svetlana Kiritchenko, Xiaodan Zhu, and Saif M Mohammad. 2014. Sentiment analysis of short informal texts. *Journal of Artificial Intelligence Research* 50:723–762.

Lun-Wei Ku and Hsin-Hsi Chen. 2007. Mining opinions from the web: Beyond relevance retrieval. *Journal of the American Society for Information Science and Technology* 58(12):1838–1850.

O. Levy, Y. Goldberg, and I Dagan. 2015. Improving distributional similarity with lessons learned from word embeddings. *Transactions of the Association for Computational Linguistics* 3:211–225.

Yanran Li, Wenjie Li, Fei Sun, and Sujian Li. 2015. Component-enhanced chinese character embeddings. In *EMNLP*. pages 829–834.

Xiangwen Liao, Binyang Li, and Liheng Xu. 2015. Overview of topic-based chinese message polarity classification in sighan 2015. In *Proceedings of the Eighth SIGHAN Workshop on Chinese Language Processing*. Beijing, China, pages 56–60.

Qiaozhu Mei, Xu Ling, Matthew Wondra, Hang Su, and ChengXiang Zhai. 2007. Topic sentiment mixture: Modeling facets and opinions in weblogs. In *Proceedings of the 16th International Conference on World Wide Web*. WWW '07, pages 171–180.

Chenggang Mi, Yating Yang, Xi Zhou, Lei Wang, Xiao Li, and Tonghai Jiang. 2016. Exploiting bishun to predict the pronunciation of chinese. *Computación y Sistemas* 20(3):541–549.

Tomas Mikolov, Ilya Sutskever, Kai Chen, Greg S Corrado, and Jeff Dean. 2013. Distributed representations of words and phrases and their compositionality. In C. J. C. Burges, L. Bottou, M. Welling, Z. Ghahramani, and K. Q. Weinberger, editors, *Advances in Neural Information Processing Systems 26*, pages 3111–3119.

Bo Pang and Lillian Lee. 2005. Seeing stars: Exploiting class relationships for sentiment categorization with respect to rating scales. In *Proceedings of the 43rd Annual Meeting on Association for Computational Linguistics*. ACL '05, pages 115–124.

Soujanya Poria, Erik Cambria, and Alexander Gelbukh. 2015. Deep convolutional neural network textual features and multiple kernel learning for utterance-level multimodal sentiment analysis. In *Proceedings of the 2015 Conference on Empirical Methods in Natural Language Processing*. pages 2539–2544.

Qiao Qian, Minlie Huang, Jinhao Lei, and Xiaoyan Zhu. 2017. Linguistically regularized lstm for sentiment classification. In *Proceedings of the 55th Annual Meeting of the Association for Computational Linguistics (Volume 1: Long Papers)*. Vancouver, Canada, pages 1679–1689.

J.A. Russell. 1980. A circumplex model of affect. *Journal of personality and social psychology* 39(6):1161–1178.

Richard Socher, Jeffrey Pennington, Eric H. Huang, Andrew Y. Ng, and Christopher D. Manning. 2011. Semi-supervised recursive autoencoders for predicting sentiment distributions. In *Proceedings of the Conference on Empirical Methods in Natural Language Processing*. EMNLP '11, pages 151–161.

Yaming Sun, Lei Lin, Duyu Tang, Nan Yang, Zhenzhou Ji, and Xiaolong Wang. 2014. Radical-enhanced chinese character embedding. *CoRR* abs/1404.4714.

Songbo Tan and Jin Zhang. 2008. An empirical study of sentiment analysis for chinese documents. *Expert Syst. Appl.* 34(4):2622–2629. https://doi.org/10.1016/j.eswa.2007.05.028.

Duyu Tang, Bing Qin, and Ting Liu. 2015. Document modeling with gated recurrent neural network for sentiment classification. In *EMNLP*. pages 1422–1432.

Xiaojun Wan. 2008. Using bilingual knowledge and ensemble techniques for unsupervised chinese sentiment analysis. In *Proceedings of the Conference on Empirical Methods in Natural Language Processing*. EMNLP '08, pages 553–561.

Janyce Wiebe and Rebecca Bruce. 1995. Probabilistic classifiers for tracking point of view. In *Proceedings of the AAAI Spring Symposium on Empirical Methods in Discourse Interpretation and Generation*. pages 181–187.

Theresa Wilson, Janyce Wiebe, and Paul Hoffmann. 2005. Recognizing contextual polarity in phrase-level sentiment analysis. In *Proceedings of the Conference on Human Language Technology and Empirical Methods in Natural Language Processing*. HLT '05, pages 347–354.

Fu Xianghua, Liu Guo, Guo Yanyan, and Wang Zhiqiang. 2013. Multi-aspect sentiment analysis for chinese online social reviews based on topic modeling and hownet lexicon. *Knowledge-Based Systems* 37:186–195.

Rongchao Yin, Quan Wang, Peng Li, Rui Li, and Bin Wang. 2016. Multi-granularity chinese word embedding. In *EMNLP*. pages 981–986.

Jinxing Yu, Xun Jian, Hao Xin, and Yangqiu Song. 2017. Joint embeddings of chinese words, characters, and fine-grained subcharacter components. In *EMNLP*.

Liang-Chih Yu, Lung-Hao Lee, Shuai Hao, Jin Wang, Yunchao He, Jun Hu, K. Robert Lai, and Xuejie Zhang. 2016a. Building chinese affective resources in valence-arousal dimensions. In *Proceedings of the 2016 Conference of the North American Chapter of the Association for Computational Linguistics: Human Language Technologies*. San Diego, California, pages 540–545.

Liang-Chih Yu, Lung-Hao Lee, and Kam-Fai Wong. 2016b. Overview of the IALP 2016 shared task on dimensional sentiment analysis for chinese words. In *2016 International Conference on Asian Language Processing, IALP*. Tainan, Taiwan, pages 156–160.

Ning Yu and Sandra Kübler. 2011. Filling the gap: Semi-supervised learning for opinion detection across domains. In *Proceedings of the Fifteenth Conference on Computational Natural Language Learning*. CoNLL '11, pages 200–209.

Changli Zhang, Daniel Zeng, Jiexun Li, Fei-Yue Wang, and Wanli Zuo. 2009. Sentiment analysis of chinese documents: From sentence to document level. *J. Am. Soc. Inf. Sci. Technol.* 60(12):2474–2487.

Jichang Zhao, Li Dong, Junjie Wu, and Ke Xu. 2012. Moodlens: An emoticon-based sentiment analysis system for chinese tweets. In *Proceedings of the 18th ACM SIGKDD International Conference on Knowledge Discovery and Data Mining*. ACM, New York, NY, USA, KDD '12, pages 1528–1531.

Chinese Answer Extraction Based on POS Tree and Genetic Algorithm

Shuihua Li, Xiaoming Zhang, Zhoujun Li
State Key Laboratory of Software Development Environment Beihang University
Beijing 100191, China
brooklsh@buaa.edu.cn

Abstract

Answer extraction is the most important part of a chinese web-based question answering system. In order to enhance the robustness and adaptability of answer extraction to new domains and eliminate the influence of the incomplete and noisy search snippets, we propose two new answer exraction methods. We utilize text patterns to generate Part-of-Speech (POS) patterns. In addition, a method is proposed to construct a POS tree by using these POS patterns. The POS tree is useful to candidate answer extraction of web-based question answering. To retrieve a efficient POS tree, the similarities between questions are used to select the question-answer pairs whose questions are similar to the unanswered question. Then, the POS tree is improved based on these question-answer pairs. In order to rank these candidate answers, the weights of the leaf nodes of the POS tree are calculated using a heuristic method. Moreover, the Genetic Algorithm (GA) is used to train the weights. The experimental results of 10-fold cross-validation show that the weighted POS tree trained by GA can improve the accuracy of answer extraction.

1 Introduction

As mature information retrieval tools, search engines can satisfy most information needs of people. But, with the rapid growth of Internet data, search engines' weakness is being revealed gradually. Traditional search engines which use keywords as input and provide a long list of HyperText Markup Language (HTML) documents are convenient for machines to run. However, Question Answering (QA) systems which use natural language as input are convenient for human beings to communicate. Some QA systems directly employ well-built search engines for this task which are called web-based QA systems (Sun et al., 2014). Most web-based QA systems have three modules: 1) question analysis module to analyze the unanswered question and generate queries which are needed for search engines; 2) search snippets retrieval module to send queries which consist of keywords to search engines and then obtain search snippets from search engines; 3) answer extraction module to extract the final answer from these search snippets. Web-based QA systems compromise the merits of search engines and QA systems: 1) the existing mature search engines enable web-based QA systems to use the abundant data on the Internet; 2) web-based QA systems can communicate with people in natural language.

At present, there are less studies on chinese web-based QA than english web-based QA. Moreover, chinese web-based QA embodies many improvements on candidate answer extraction and ranking. We focus on answer extraction of chinese web-based QA system which can answer factoid questions. In order to enhance the robustness and adaptability of answer extraction to new domains and eliminate the influence of the incomplete and noisy search snippets, we propose two answer exraction methods based on POS tree.

The similarities between questions are used to select the question-answer pairs whose questions are similar to the unanswered question. These question-answer pairs are utilized to generate text patterns which can be transformed to POS patterns. Then, we propose a method to construct a POS tree using these POS patterns. The POS tree is of use to candidate answer extraction of web-based QA. To rank candidate answers, we use a heuristic method to calculate the weights of the

Proceedings of the 9th SIGHAN Workshop on Chinese Language Processing, pages 30–36,
Taipei, Taiwan, December 1, 2017. ©2017 AFNLP

POS tree's leaf nodes. Moreover, the Genetic Algorithm (GA) (Andrew, 1993) is used to train the weights. The results of the experiments show that the weighted POS tree trained by GA can improve the accuracy of answer extraction.

Our contributions in the paper are three-fold: 1) proposal of a new chinese answer extraction method based on POS tree; 2) proposal of a training method for POS tree by using GA; 3) empirical verification of the proposed methods.

The remainder of this paper is organized as follows: in section 2, we will discuss about related work. In section 3, a method to construct a POS tree and another method to train the POS tree with GA will be presented in detail. In section 4, the experimental results of 10-fold cross-validation will be shown. In section 5, this paper will be concluded.

2 Related Work

Answer extraction is the most difficult part of a web-based QA system. As such, it is also the focus of this paper.

Traditional web-based QA systems typically use search snippets directly (Brill et al., 2001; Sun et al., 2015). Although plain texts in the retrieved HTML documents can offer more information (Ravichandran and Hovy, 2002; Liu et al., 2014), the search snippets as high-quality summarizations generated by search engines can save web-based QA systems from having to crawl, parse and filter HTML documents. In spite of efficiency improved by search engines, they lead to another problem: some state-of-the-art answer extraction methods (Severyn and Moschitti, 2013; Yao et al., 2013; Liu et al., 2014) rely on syntactic information cound be seriously affected by these search snippets which consis of incomplete sentences.

The process of extracting a final answer from the search snippets has two steps: 1) extract candidate answers such as names, dates and places, and so on; 2) rank these candidate answers based on ranking method to find the best one as the final answer. There are many candidate answer extraction methods, such as: 1) some work use dictionaries which are edited manually or generated automatically to generate candidate answers. For example, the famous QA system Watson (Chu-Carroll and Fan, 2011) extracts titles from Wikipedia entries as candidate answers. This method provides a large candidate answer set which requests lots of effort for maintaining, updating and ranking. Besides, this method has low adaptability to new domains. 2) The most commonly adopted method is to use Named Entity Recognition (NER) tools to extract Named Entity (NE) that matching with question type (Xu et al., 2003). This method is always used together with question type classification algorithm. The performance of this method will be limited by the performance of classification algorithm and NER tools. 3) Another commonly used method is to etract candidate answers with text patterns which are edited manually or generated automatically (Zhang and Lee, 2002; Bhagat and Ravichandran, 2008; Khashabi et al., 2016). This method has high precision. However, these text patterns are too fine-grained to be adapted to new data.

There are also many ranking methods which can choose a best answer from a candidate answer set, such as: 1) a simple and commonly used method is to rank candidate answers by the similarities between candidate answers and the unanswered question in Vector Space Model (VSM). This method can be used with Latent Semantic Analysis and word2vec tool (Mikolov et al., 2013). 2) Another commonly used method is to compute the similarities by syntactic information. To improve performance of this method, tree edit distance (Severyn and Moschitti, 2013) and factor graph (Sun et al., 2013) can be used. 3) Some work rank candidate answers by a combination of features, e.g., lexical features, semantic features, statistical features and similarity features, and so on (Severyn and Moschitti, 2013; Khodadi and Abadeh, 2016). For comprehensive utilization of these features, some global optimization algorithms such as GA are needed (Figueroa and Neumann, 2008).

3 Method

We have implemented a chinese web-based QA system. In this section, we will discuss our answer extraction method of the system in detail below. The method contains three steps: 1) construct a POS tree using POS patterns generated by the question-answer pairs whose questions are similar to the unanswered question; 2) train the weights of the leaf nodes of the POS tree; 3) extract and rank candidate answers with the trained POS tree to find the best answer.

Item Name	Item Value
question Q	北大校长是谁?
keywords of Q	北大, 校长
answer A	林建华
search snippet S	...中组部宣布林建华担任北大校长，王恩哥不再担任北大校长...
target substring S^*	林建华担任北大校长
segmentation of S^*	林建华/nr 担任/v 北大/j 校长/n
POS pattern P	nr#a v j#k n#k#e

Table 1: An example of extraction of a POS pattern.

3.1 POS Tree

Extension of POS: Given a word w, define $t(w)$ as its extension of POS. In addition to POS, $t(w)$ may have some of three different marks: 1) mark #a means w is a part of the answer; 2) mark #k means w is a keyword of the question; 3) mark #e means w is the last word of a pattern.

POS Pattern: Given an answered question Q and its answer A, if there is a search snippet S contains A and some keywords of Q, then there is a shortest substring S^* of S also contains A and some keywords of Q. We name S^* as target substring. If segmentation of S^* is $(s_1, s_2, ..., s_n)$, then we get a POS pattern $P = (t(s_1), t(s_2), ..., t(s_n))$.

POS patterns that are abstracted from text patterns have better adaptability. An example of exraction of a POS pattern is shown in Table 1. The extract POS pattern algorithm is shown in Algorithm 1.

Algorithm 1 Extract POS Pattern

Input: question's keywords K, answer A and search snippet S

Output: POS pattern P

```
if S contains K and A then
    S* ⇐ target substring of S
    P ⇐ ()
    for each word w in S* do
        append t(w) to P
    end for
end if
```

POS Tree: Given a POS pattern set L, we can construct a POS tree T which cover every POS pattern of L. T consists of extension of POS but excudes the root node. Every path from the root node to a leaf node in T represents a POS pattern in L.

To construct a POS tree, we need some question-answer pairs whose questions are similar to the unanswered question, because we believe that the more similar a couple of questions are, the more likely they will both match a POS pattern. To find these question-answer pairs, we transform questions to vectors with word2vec tool, then classify the unanswered question with Support Vector Machine (SVM) (Suykens and Vandewalle, 1999) and compute its cosine similarties between questions of all question-answer pairs of its category. In addition, the POS tree can not be cached, but those POS patterns can. Those cached POS patterns can speed up the construction of another POS tree. An example of a POS pattern set is shown in Table 2. For this example, the POS tree we can construct is shown in Figure 1(a). The construct POS tree algorithm is shown in Algorithm 2.

Target Substring	POS pattern
林建华担任北大校长	nr#a v j#k n#k#e
林建华挂帅北大	nr#a v j#k#e
北大新任校长林建华	j#k b n#k nr#a#e
北大校长是林建华	j#k n#k v nr#a#e
北大校长林建华	j#k n#k nr#a#e

Table 2: An example of a POS pattern set.

Algorithm 2 Construct POS Tree

Input: POS pattern set L

Output: POS tree T

```
add root node N_ROOT to T
for P ∈ L do
    N_NOW ⇐ N_ROOT
    for each t(w) in P do
        if N_NOW doesn't has a t(w) child then
            create a t(w) child for N_NOW
        end if
        N_NOW ⇐ the t(w) child of N_NOW
    end for
end for
```

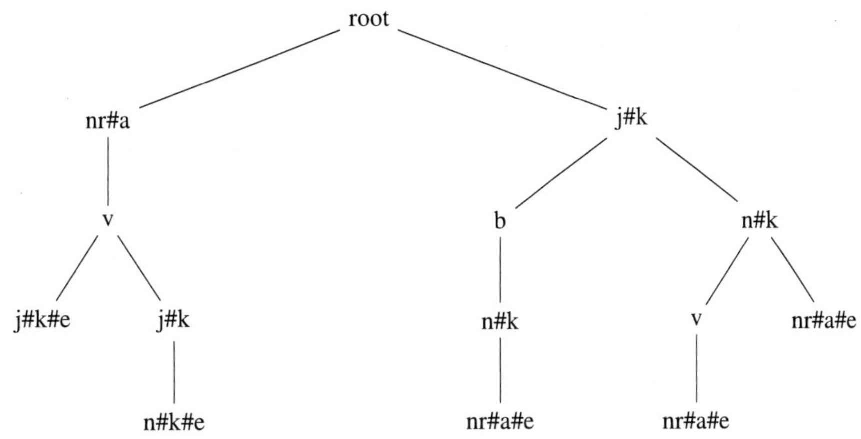

(a) Before the answer extraction process.

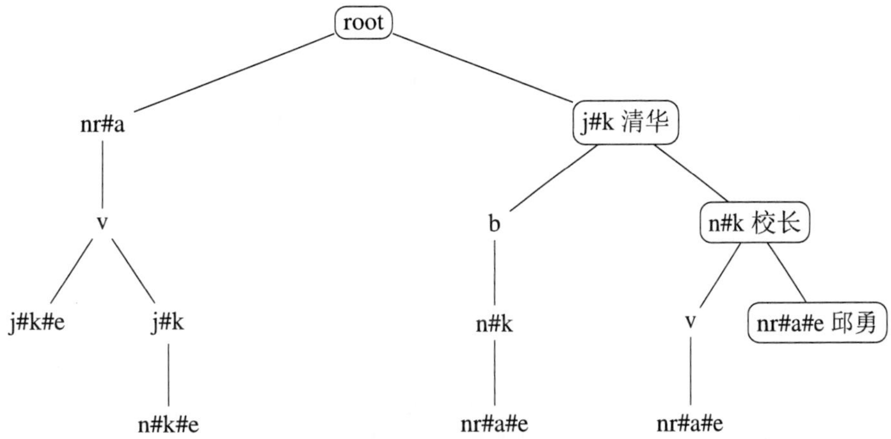

(b) During the answer extraction process.

Figure 1: An example of a POS tree.

3.2 Candidate Answer Extraction Based on POS Tree

When a new question Q is submited, we can extract its keywords K and get a search snippet set X about it. For each search snippet S in X, the segmentation of S can be used to extract candidate answers with the POS tree T that we have constructed before.

For the example question Q in Table 3 and the POS tree T in Figure 1(a), we can extract candidate answer like Figure 1(b) and then we get a candidate answer "邱勇".

3.3 Train POS Tree and Rank Candidate Answers

In the previous subsection, we discussed how to extract candidate answers with a POS tree. However, people only need a best answer instead of many equally important candidate answers. To rank these candidate answers, the weights of the leaf nodes of the POS tree are calculated. The score of a candidate answer would be the sum over all the weighs of the leaf nodes which contribute to the generation process of this candidate answer. Then we rank these candidate answers by their score to choose the final answer.

Every leaf node of the POS tree corresponds to a POS pattern. So, there is a simple heuristic method to calculate weights of these leaf nodes: just set the weight of a leaf node to the number of POS patterns it corresponds to. These POS patterns are extracted from the question-answer pairs while we are constructing the POS tree. This method does work well. The experimental results of this method will be shown in the next section.

In addition, we use GA to train the weights of

Item Name	Item Value
question Q	清华校长是谁?
keywords of Q	清华, 校长
search snippet S	...2016年，清华校长邱勇毕业致辞...
segmentation of S	...2016/m 年/q ，/w 清华/j 校长/n 邱勇/nr 毕业/v 致辞/v ...

Table 3: A new question.

Algorithm 3 Train POS Tree

Input: POS tree T and similar question set V of the new question
Output: trained POS tree T

```
initialize population P_NOW which consists of random genes, every gene is a weight array for a leaf
node of T.
G_BEST ⇐ a random gene
while the number of iterations is less than the threshold do
    for G ∈ P_NOW do
        set the weights of the leaf nodes of T to G
        set the fitness of G to MRR which computed using T and V
        if the fitness of G is higher than the fitness of G_BEST then
            G_BEST ⇐ G
        end if
    end for
    if the fitness of G_BEST is equals to the max fitness then
        break while
    end if
    P_NEXT ⇐ ∅
    while |P_NEXT| < |P_NOW| do
        get two gene G_1 and G_2 by roulette selection from P_NOW
        cross or mutate G_1 and G_2 in a certain probability
        add G_1 and G_2 to P_NEXT
    end while
    P_NOW ⇐ P_NEXT
end while
set the weights of the leaf nodes of T to G_BEST
```

the leaf nodes. Every gene that used in GA is a weight array. Train data of GA is those question-answer pairs which are used to construct the POS tree. The fitness function of GA is Mean Reciprocal Rank (MRR) of the ranked candidate answers which are extracted from these question-answer pairs with the POS tree and a gene. The MRR is the average of the reciprocal ranks of the ranked candidate answers for n question-answer pairs:

$$MRR = \frac{1}{n}\sum_{i=1}^{n}\frac{1}{rank_i} \qquad (1)$$

where $rank_i$ refers to the rank position of the first relevant candidate answer for the i-th question-answer pair. The train pos tree algorithm is shown in Algorithm 3.

While the web-based QA system is constructing a POS tree, it can retrieval search snippets for the unanswered question at the same time. When the POS tree and these search snippets are both ready, the best answer can be extracted from these search snippets with the POS tree. Then, the system will return a best answer or top k ranked candidate answers with sentences based on the circumstances.

4 Experiments

Finally, in order to verify the effectiveness of our methods, we have built a question-answer dataset with 256 question-answer pairs artificially. There are five question types in this dataset: WHO,

Method	MRR of WHOs	MRR of WHENs	MRR of WHEREs	MRR of HOW MANYs	MRR of WHATs	MRR
NER	**0.6965**	0.4130	0.5610	0.5681	0.3102	0.5911
Simple POS tree	0.6943	0.6621	0.6319	0.4621	**0.5762**	0.6538
POS tree & GA	0.6051	**0.7422**	**0.7226**	**0.5758**	0.5458	**0.6615**

(a) On baidu data

Method	MRR of WHOs	MRR of WHENs	MRR of WHEREs	MRR of HOW MANYs	MRR of WHATs	MRR
NER	0.6756	0.3676	0.4762	0.4696	0.3444	0.5431
Simple POS tree	**0.6780**	0.6207	0.6144	0.4697	0.5213	0.6334
POS tree & GA	0.6053	**0.6579**	**0.6986**	**0.5182**	**0.5833**	**0.6409**

(b) On bing data

Table 4: The results of 10-fold cross-validation

Question/Method	WHO	WHEN	WHERE	NUM	WHAT
Question	洛神赋 是谁写的	平安夜是 什么时候	泰山在 哪个省	金庸写了 多少部小说	熊猫 吃什么
NER	1.曹植 2.甄姬 3.甄洛	1.2015年 2.2014年 3.12月24日	1.华山 2.山东 3.泰安	1.一 2.15 3.几	1.大熊猫 2.竹子 3.熊猫兔
Simple POS tree	1.曹植 2.顾恺之 3.张渊书	1.12月24日 2.12月25日 3.11月28日	1.山东 2.山东省 3.黄山	1.15 2.一 3.十四	1.竹子 2.粪便 3.杂食
POS tree & GA	1.曹植 2.顾恺之 3.甄宓	1.12月24日 2.12月25日 3.2016年12月24日	1.山东 2.山东省 3.泰安市	1.15 2.14 3.十四	1.竹子 2.又名 3.观赏鱼

Table 5: Some examples of experimental results.

WHEN, WHERE, HOW MANY, WHAT. For every question-answer pair, we have retrieved 100 search snippets from two popular search engines, baidu and bing.

In this paper, we experiment our two methods compared with the commonly used method, NER based method. The results of 10-fold cross-validation on baidu data is shown in Table 4(a) and on bing data is shown in Table 4(b). The heuristic method which is proposed in previous section is named "Simple POS tree", and the method with GA is named "POS tree & GA" in experimental results. From Table 4(a) and Table 4(b), we could see that our methods are better than the NER based method expect the WHO questions. We think the cause might be that the NER based method is good at name recognition but weak in recognition of other categories. The experimental results also show that GA can imporve the POS tree method. Our methods' performance on some pretty specific questions are shown in Table 5.

5 Conclusion

Web-based QA systems can extract a final answer from search snippets which are retrieved from search engines for an unanswered question. Answer extraction is the most important and difficult part of a chinese web-based QA system, because there are many incomplete and noisy sentences in these search snippets. In order to enhance the robustness and adaptability of answer extraction to new domains and eliminate the influence of the incomplete and noisy search snippets, we propose two new answer exraction methods. We utilize text patterns to generate POS patterns, then use POS patterns to construct a POS tree. The POS tree can be used to extract candidate answers from these search snippets. To rank these candidate answers, we propose a heuristic method and another method with GA. The results of 10-fold cross-validation show that the two methods work well and the weighted POS tree that trained by GA can improve the accuracy of answer extraction.

References

Alex M. Andrew. 1993. *Systems: An Introductory Analysis with Applications to Biology, Control, and Artificial Intelligence*, by john h. holland MIT press (bradford books), cambridge, mass., 1992, xiv+211 pp. (paperback £13.50, cloth £26.95). *Robotica*, 11(5):489.

Rahul Bhagat and Deepak Ravichandran. 2008. Large scale acquisition of paraphrases for learning surface patterns. In *ACL 2008, Proceedings of the 46th Annual Meeting of the Association for Computational Linguistics, June 15-20, 2008, Columbus, Ohio, USA*, pages 674–682.

Eric Brill, Jimmy J. Lin, Michele Banko, Susan T. Dumais, and Andrew Y. Ng. 2001. Data-intensive question answering. In *Proceedings of The Tenth Text REtrieval Conference, TREC 2001, Gaithersburg, Maryland, USA, November 13-16, 2001*.

Jennifer Chu-Carroll and James Fan. 2011. Leveraging wikipedia characteristics for search and candidate generation in question answering. In *Proceedings of the Twenty-Fifth AAAI Conference on Artificial Intelligence, AAAI 2011, San Francisco, California, USA, August 7-11, 2011*.

Alejandro Figueroa and Günter Neumann. 2008. Genetic algorithms for data-driven web question answering. *Evolutionary Computation*, 16(1):89–125.

Daniel Khashabi, Tushar Khot, Ashish Sabharwal, Peter Clark, Oren Etzioni, and Dan Roth. 2016. Question answering via integer programming over semi-structured knowledge. In *Proceedings of the Twenty-Fifth International Joint Conference on Artificial Intelligence, IJCAI 2016, New York, NY, USA, 9-15 July 2016*, pages 1145–1152.

Iman Khodadi and Mohammad Saniee Abadeh. 2016. Genetic programming-based feature learning for question answering. *Inf. Process. Manage.*, 52(2):340–357.

Zengjian Liu, Xiao-Long Wang, Qingcai Chen, Yaoyun Zhang, and Yang Xiang. 2014. A chinese question answering system based on web search. In *2014 International Conference on Machine Learning and Cybernetics, Lanzhou, China, July 13-16, 2014*, pages 816–820.

Tomas Mikolov, Ilya Sutskever, Kai Chen, Gregory S. Corrado, and Jeffrey Dean. 2013. Distributed representations of words and phrases and their compositionality. In *Advances in Neural Information Processing Systems 26: 27th Annual Conference on Neural Information Processing Systems 2013. Proceedings of a meeting held December 5-8, 2013, Lake Tahoe, Nevada, United States.*, pages 3111–3119.

Deepak Ravichandran and Eduard H. Hovy. 2002. Learning surface text patterns for a question answering system. In *Proceedings of the 40th Annual Meeting of the Association for Computational Linguistics, July 6-12, 2002, Philadelphia, PA, USA.*, pages 41–47.

Aliaksei Severyn and Alessandro Moschitti. 2013. Automatic feature engineering for answer selection and extraction. In *Proceedings of the 2013 Conference on Empirical Methods in Natural Language Processing, EMNLP 2013, 18-21 October 2013, Grand Hyatt Seattle, Seattle, Washington, USA, A meeting of SIGDAT, a Special Interest Group of the ACL*, pages 458–467.

Hong Sun, Nan Duan, Yajuan Duan, and Ming Zhou. 2013. Answer extraction from passage graph for question answering. In *IJCAI 2013, Proceedings of the 23rd International Joint Conference on Artificial Intelligence, Beijing, China, August 3-9, 2013*, pages 2169–2175.

Hong Sun, Furu Wei, and Ming Zhou. 2014. Answer extraction with multiple extraction engines for web-based question answering. In *Natural Language Processing and Chinese Computing - Third CCF Conference, NLPCC 2014, Shenzhen, China, December 5-9, 2014. Proceedings*, pages 321–332.

Huan Sun, Hao Ma, Wen-tau Yih, Chen-Tse Tsai, Jingjing Liu, and Ming-Wei Chang. 2015. Open domain question answering via semantic enrichment. In *Proceedings of the 24th International Conference on World Wide Web, WWW 2015, Florence, Italy, May 18-22, 2015*, pages 1045–1055.

Johan A. K. Suykens and Joos Vandewalle. 1999. Least squares support vector machine classifiers. *Neural Processing Letters*, 9(3):293–300.

Jinxi Xu, Ana Licuanan, Jonathan May, Scott Miller, and Ralph M. Weischedel. 2003. Answer selection and confidence estimation. In *New Directions in Question Answering, Papers from 2003 AAAI Spring Symposium, Stanford University, Stanford, CA, USA*, pages 134–137.

Xuchen Yao, Benjamin Van Durme, Chris Callison-Burch, and Peter Clark. 2013. Answer extraction as sequence tagging with tree edit distance. In *Human Language Technologies: Conference of the North American Chapter of the Association of Computational Linguistics, Proceedings, June 9-14, 2013, Westin Peachtree Plaza Hotel, Atlanta, Georgia, USA*, pages 858–867.

Dell Zhang and Wee Sun Lee. 2002. Web based pattern mining and matching approach to question answering. In *Proceedings of The Eleventh Text REtrieval Conference, TREC 2002, Gaithersburg, Maryland, USA, November 19-22, 2002*.

Learning from Parenthetical Sentences for Term Translation in Machine Translation

Guoping Huang and **Jiajun Zhang** and **Yu Zhou** and **Chengqing Zong**
National Laboratory of Pattern Recognition,
Institute of Automation, Chinese Academy of Sciences, Beijing, China
{guoping.huang, jjzhang, yzhou, cqzong}@nlpr.ia.ac.cn

Abstract

Terms extensively exist in specific domains, and term translation plays a critical role in domain-specific machine translation (MT) tasks. However, it's a challenging task to translate them correctly for the huge number of pre-existing terms and the endless new terms. To achieve better term translation quality, it is necessary to inject external term knowledge into the underlying MT system. Fortunately, there are plenty of term translation knowledge in parenthetical sentences on the Internet. In this paper, we propose a simple, straightforward and effective framework to improve term translation by learning from parenthetical sentences. This framework includes: (1) a focused web crawler; (2) a parenthetical sentence filter, acquiring parenthetical sentences including bilingual term pairs; (3) a term translation knowledge extractor, extracting bilingual term translation candidates; (4) a probability learner, generating the term translation table for MT decoders. The extensive experiments demonstrate that our proposed framework significantly improves the translation quality of terms and sentences.

1 Introduction

Terms, the linguistic representation of concepts, a noun or compound word used in a specific context, deliver essential context and meaning in human languages, such as "interprocess communication" or abbreviated as "IPC". In this paper, we do not consider named entities (e.g., person names, location names, organization names, time and numbers). Terms extensively exist in specific domains. For example, in Microsoft Translation Memory, there are 8 terms out of every 100 words, whereas names entities are nearly nonexistent. What's more, new terms are being created all the time, such as in areas of computer science and medicine. Thus, term translation plays a critical role in domain-specific tasks of machine translations (MT), especially statistical machine translation (SMT).

However, unlike person names or other named entities having obvious characteristics and boundary clues, it's a challenging task to translate terms correctly for the huge number of pre-existing terms and the endless new terms. In practice, to achieve better term translation quality, it is necessary to inject external term knowledge into the underlying MT system. The best way is to import a bilingual technical term dictionary, such as such as Microsoft Terminology [1]. But the high cost makes it impossible to construct such bilingual dictionary by human experts for various domains. Thus how to learning bilingual term knowledge automatically becomes the key of term translation in domain-specific MT tasks.

The state-of-art term translation knowledge extraction methods tend to take the Internet as a big corpus (Ren et al., 2010). The most important assumption behind these methods is that the corresponding translation for every source term must exist somewhere on the web. Then, the term translation pair extraction problem is converted to the task of finding these translations from the web and extract them correctly. As a result, except terms, the other various fragments, including multi-word expressions , will be extracted for the lack of term recognization. Not surprisingly, it has increased system workloads and directly reduces the quality of term translation.

[1] https://www.microsoft.com/Language/en-us/default.aspx

Proceedings of the 9th SIGHAN Workshop on Chinese Language Processing, pages 37–45,
Taipei, Taiwan, December 1, 2017. ©2017 AFNLP

Example 1: A parenthetical sentence
不过 各个 进程 有 自己 的 内存 空间 、 数据 栈 等 ， 所以 只能 使用 进程 间 通讯 (interprocess communication , IPC) ， 而 不能 直接 共享 信息 。

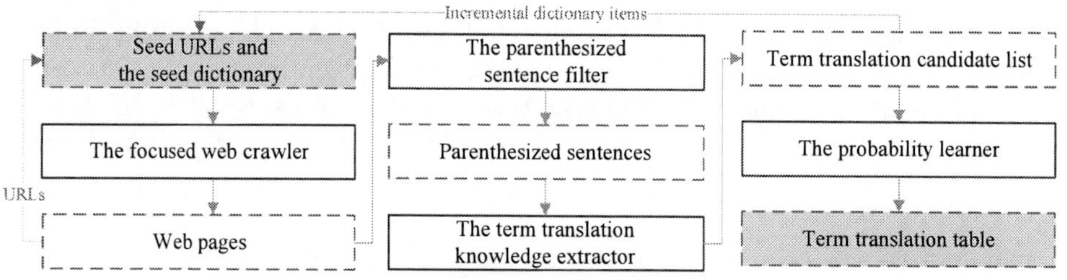

Figure 1: An overview of learning from parenthetical sentences for term translation.

For the extraction of term translation knowledge, we should put quality before quantity. Thus, in this paper, we turn to parenthetical sentences in mix-language web pages for acquiring term translation knowledge. In this work, a sentence will be called **parenthetical sentence** when the following conditions are true: (1) the sentence contains one or more parentheses; (2) the phrase immediately to the left of the parenthesis is a term; (3) the corresponding translation of the term is included in the parenthesis. The parenthetical sentence can be denoted as $s = c_1c_2 \dots c_n(e_1e_2 \dots e_m)$, where $c_1c_2 \dots c_n$ is a Chinese term and $e_1e_2 \dots e_m$ is its corresponding English translation. In this paper, the term included in the parenthesis and out of parentheses are referred to *source term* $(e_1e_2 \dots e_m)$ and *target term* $(c_1c_2 \dots c_n)$, respectively. A typical parenthetical sentence is shown as following Example 1.

In Example 1, the Chinese sentence contains one parenthesis, the phrase "进程 间 通讯" immediately to the left of the parenthesis is a target term, and the corresponding source term is "interprocess communication" or abbreviated as "IPC". Therefore, it is a parenthetical sentence.

There are plenty of term translation knowledge in parenthetical sentences. Compared with parallel/comparable sentences, parenthetical sentences have fewer limits, update quickly and are easy to obtain. As we can see in Example 1, the main task for extracting the correct bilingual term pairs is to find the left boundary of the target term. Most importantly, the bilingual term pairs in parenthetical sentences have greater quality compared to other text in various web pages.

In this paper, in order to achieve high accuracy, we propose a simple and effective framework to improve term translation by learning from parenthetical sentences. The proposed framework includes: (1) a focused web crawler, fetching and parsing relevant pages selectively; (2) a parenthetical sentence filter, acquiring parenthetical sentences including bilingual term pairs; (3) a term translation knowledge extractor, extracting bilingual term translation candidates; (4) a probability learner, generating the term translation table for MT decoders.

An overview of the proposed framework is shown in Figure 1. The input includes seed URLs and the seed dictionary. The final result is the term translation table with probabilities, being similar to phrase translation table in MT. In the processing flow, the intermediate results include the crawled web pages, extracted URLs, the filtered parenthetical sentences, the extracted incremental dictionary items and the extracted term translation candidate list. The key steps include identifying the left boundaries of target terms by employing a maximal entropy classifier, and generating the probabilities of items as shown in Example 2, in the term translation table in cooperating with SMT system. In this paper, we regard the term translation table as a feature of MT decoders.

During decoding in the sentence translation tasks, translation hypotheses are searched both in the phrase translation table and in the generated term translation table. The underlying MT decoder gets the scores of hypotheses from both tables, and selects the n-best list among translation hypotheses.

In the experiments, our proposed novel framework significantly improves the translation quality

Example 2: The term translation table based on Example 1

communication ||| 通信 ||| 0.387201 0.358436 0.623309 0.668845 ||| 0-0
interprocess ||| 间 ||| 0.00358423 0.0028275 0.333333 0.6 ||| 0-0
interprocess ||| 进程 间 ||| 0.333333 0.00160575 0.666667 0.24 ||| 0-0 0-1
interprocess communication ||| 间 通信 ||| 0.333333 0.000101348 0.333333 0.401307 ||| 0-0 1-1
interprocess communication ||| 进程 间 通信 ||| 0.4 0.000575558 0.666667 0.160523 ||| 0-0 0-1 1-2
IPC ||| 间 通信 ||| 0.333333 0.416858 0.0454545 0.352726 ||| 0-0 0-1
IPC ||| 进程 间 通信 ||| 0.65625 0.731707 0.5 0.120435 ||| 0-0 0-1 0-2

of terms and sentences. In summary, this paper makes the following contributions:

(1) The proposed simple and straightforward framework gets more reliable and accurate term translation knowledge by learning from parenthetical sentences. It substantially improves the translation quality of terms and sentences.

(2) The proposed framework regards the term translation table as a feature of MT decoders. It allows term translation knowledge to be more fully utilized compared with traditional bilingual term dictionaries.

(3) The well designed term translation knowledge extractor continuously extracts term translation candidates from parenthetical sentences. Some of the extracted candidates will be added into the seed dictionary as incremental dictionary items, so as to improve the accuracy of parenthetical sentences.

2 The Proposed Framework

In this section, we first introduce the whole framework, then give a detailed description of this framework in the following subsections.

The primary insight of the proposed framework is that authors of many mix-language web pages, especially non-English pages (such as Chinese, Japanese), usually annotate terms with their original English translations insides of a pair of parentheses. Thus we can extract some term translation pairs follow parenthesis pattern, especially for technical terms.

To achieve better term translation quality, our proposed framework includes four parts as shown in Figure 1:

(1) A focused web crawler, collecting relevant web pages. Different from general purpose crawlers, the crawler employed by this paper is a focused crawler, collecting web pages that contain parenthetical sentences. The proposed focused crawler will predict the probability that an unvisited page contains parenthetical sentences before actually downloading the page.

(2) A parenthetical sentence filter, acquiring parenthetical sentences including bilingual term pairs. There are various proposes of parenthesis patterns, such as term translation, explanation, supplement, examples. The proposed filter picks out sentences that contain only term translation and match the parenthesis pattern. Then parenthetical sentences will be acquired.

(3) A term translation knowledge extractor, extracting bilingual term translation candidates. The extractor identifies the left boundaries of target terms by employing a maximal entropy classifier. Then, the term translation candidate list for the parenthesized source term is extracted depending on the left anchor, namely the given left boundary. The classifier was trained by naturally annotated resources (e.g., Wikipedia) and the seed dictionary.

(4) A probability learner, generating the term translation table for MT decoders. Instead of extracting a multipurpose bilingual dictionary for many applications, in this paper, we design a probability learner to generate the term translation table with probabilities in cooperating with MT decoders. The learned probabilities help MT decoders achieve better translation quality compared with that of using bilingual term dictionary directly.

2.1 Focused Crawler

Crawlers used by general purpose search engines retrieve massive numbers of web pages regardless of their content. However, there are various kinds of web pages on the Internet, and only a small fraction of pages happens to contain parenthetical sentences. So, the focused crawler (Pal et al., 2009) is employed in this paper to collect targeted pages, by carefully prioritizing the crawl frontier and managing the hyperlink exploration process.

The proposed focused crawler in this paper will predict the probability that an unvisited page contains parenthetical sentences before actually downloading this page. The larger the probability, the higher the visiting priority will be assigned to the URL in the task queue.

A URL consists of the *domain*, the *path* and other parts. For instance, given the URL "https://en.wikipedia.org/wiki/Memory", the domain is "en.wikipedia.org" and the path is "/wiki/Memory". We assume that a page may contain more parenthetical sentences if: (1) other pages in the same domain have more parenthetical sentences; (2) the parent page from which the URL is extracted contains many parenthetical sentences. Therefore, the probability that a URL contains parenthetical sentences is calculated by:

$$\log p(url) = 0.5 \times \log \frac{count(url.domain)}{total(url.domain)} + 0.5 \times \log \frac{count(url.parent)}{total(url.parent)} \quad (1)$$

where *count* refers to the number of parenthetical sentences, and *total* refers to the number of sentences. The value of *count* is given by the parenthetical sentence filter introduced in the next subsection. The focused crawler reorders the task queue by the probability according to Equation 1.

A Bloom filter is employed for filtering duplicate URLs, and the controlled Chromium browser is adopted to simulate keyboard and mouse actions for downloading pages which cannot be accessed in the general way.

2.2 Parenthetical Sentence Filter

There are various proposes of parenthesis patterns, such as term translation, explanation, supplement, and demonstration. Several typical parenthesis patterns are shown in Example 3. Only the patterns for term translation are focused in this paper, and other patterns should be eliminated.

In order to acquire parenthetical sentences for learning term translation, we design a parenthetical sentence filter to identify whether a sentence matching the parenthesis pattern should be retained or not. For a parenthetical sentence $s = c_1c_2\ldots c_n(e_1e_2\ldots e_m)$, the proposed filter combines the seed dictionary, co-occurrence and predefined rules to score the parenthetical sentence candidate according to the following equation:

$$\log p(s) = \lambda_1 \log p(domain) + \lambda_2 \log p(page) + \lambda_3 \log r(s) + \lambda_4 \log co(s) \quad (2)$$

In Equation 2, $r(s)$ refers to the ratio of source words that correspond to target words according to the dictionary can be matched before the left parenthesis and can be calculated by the following equations:

$$r(s) = \frac{1}{m} \times \sum_{j=1}^{m} sign(e_j) \quad (3)$$

$$sign(e_j) = \begin{cases} 0 & \forall\, t' \in dict(e_j),\ t' \notin \{c_n\} \\ 1 & \exists\, t' \in dict(e_j),\ t' \in \{c_n\} \end{cases} \quad (4)$$

where $dict(e_j)$ refers to the target word set of the source word e_j according to the seed dictionary.

In Equation 2, $co(s)$ denotes the average co-frequency of source words and target words and can be calculated by the following equation:

$$co(s) = \frac{1}{m} \times \sum_{j=1}^{m} \max_{1\le i\le n, e_j\in s, c_i\in s} \frac{2 \times count(e_j, c_i)}{count(e_j) + count(c_i)} \quad (5)$$

After analysis, there are some typical websites and pages containing an especially great number of bilingual pairs. Such prior information is very helpful to recognize parenthetical sentences. Thus, in Equation 2, $s(domain)$ denotes the probability of one sentence included in *domain* contains parenthetical term translation and can be derived as the following equation:

$$s(domain) = \frac{1}{|domain|} \sum_{s'\in domain} \left(\frac{\lambda_3 \times r(s')}{\lambda_3 + \lambda_4} + \frac{\lambda_4 \times co(s')}{\lambda_3 + \lambda_4} \right) \quad (6)$$

where $|domain|$ refers to the number of sentences in this domain. Similarly, the probability of one

Example 3: Several typical parenthesis patterns
Term translation: 软件开发中的**焦油坑**(the tar pit)可以通过尽责、专业的过程得以避免。 岩石里有种构造叫**夫妻节理**(英文：coupled joints)
Explanation: 蓟北：泛指蓟州、幽州一带(现在河北省北部地区)，是安、史叛军盘踞的地方。
Supplement: **艾米莉·狄金森**(1830-1886)是美国文学史上一个伟大的诗人。 **斯巴达克**(杀开一条血路，大喊)不愿做奴隶的人们！起来！
Demonstration: 从图中两组节理面的**锐角**(beta)可计算出该岩石的内摩擦 转载请注意说明**来源**(www.qq.com) 没有被收录在词表中的词，包括各类**专有名词**(人名、地名、企业名等)

sentence included in $page$ contains parenthetical term translation, $s(page)$, can be derived as the following equation:

$$s(page) = \frac{1}{|page|} \sum_{s' \in page} \left(\frac{\lambda_3 \times r(s')}{\lambda_3 + \lambda_4} + \frac{\lambda_4 \times co(s')}{\lambda_3 + \lambda_4} \right) \quad (7)$$

where $|page|$ refers to the number of sentences in this page.

In this paper, the default values of λ are set to the following weights: $\lambda_1 = \lambda_2 = 0.2$, $\lambda_3 = \lambda_4 = 0.3$.

2.3 Term Translation Knowledge Extractor

In order to extract bilingual term translation candidates, the key task is to identify the left boundary of a target term. However, traditional term recognition methods employing statistical measures to rand the candidates terms (n-gram sequences), such as log likelihood (Cohen, 1995; Lefever et al., 2009), TF-IDF (Evans and Lefferts, 1995; Medelyan and Witten, 2006), C-value/NC-value (Frantzi et al., 2000) and many others (Ahmad et al., 2000; Park et al., 2002; Kozakov et al., 2004; Sclano and Velardi, 2007; Zhou et al., 2008; Zhang et al., 2008; Kostoff et al., 2009), leads to very low recall for some domains. What's worse, some approaches apply frequency threshold to reduce the algorithm's search space by filtering out low frequency term candidates. Such methods have not taken into account Zipf's law, again leading to the reduced recall.

In this paper, to achieve a higher recall, we adopt naturally annotated resources for term recognition and focus on supervised machine learning approaches based recognition approaches for MT with a wide range of fields. Thus, we train a maximal entropy based term recognition model using Wikipedia sentences to detect the left boundary candidate of a given target term.

There are plenty of naturally annotated resources with parenthetical sentences that can be used to train the term recognizer as shown in Figure 2, especially Wikipedia. In Figure 2, the phrases with red rectangles are terms. As we can see, this terms are naturally annotated with bold fonts or hyperlinks. And such natural annotations clearly provide the important boundary information of terms and can be adopted as training data of term recognizers.

In this paper, we design following features for the term recognizer: the four words immediately to the left of the term, $W_{s-4}, \ldots, W_{s-1}$, and their parts of speech, $POS_{s-4}, \ldots, POS_{s-1}$; the four words immediately to the right of the term $W_{s+1}, \ldots, W_{s+4}$, and their parts of speech, $POS_{s+1}, \ldots, POS_{s+4}$; the first word of the phrase WL and the part of speech $POSL$; the last word of the phrase WR and the part of speech $POSR$; the ratio of target words, D, that match parenthetical source words according to the seed dictionary.

In this way, we can get the probability $p(c_i)$ of an anchor, the first word of the term. Then, the term translation candidate list for the parenthesized source term is extracted depending on the left anchor. An example of extracted English-Chinese term translation candidates is shown in Table 1.

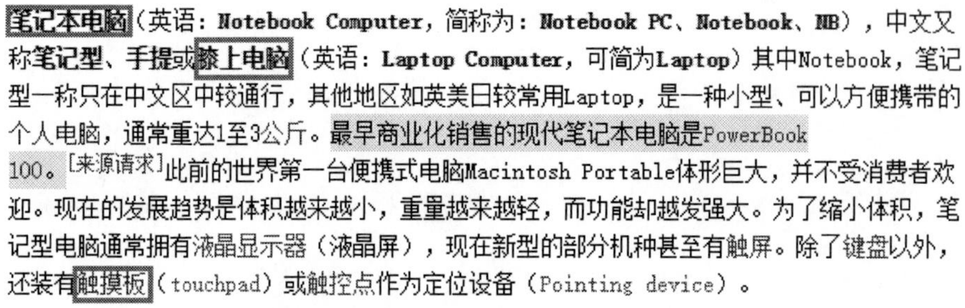
笔记本电脑（英语：Notebook Computer，简称为：Notebook PC、Notebook、NB），中文又称笔记型、手提或膝上电脑（英语：Laptop Computer，可简为Laptop）其中Notebook，笔记型一称只在中文区中较通行，其他地区如英美日较常用Laptop，是一种小型、可以方便携带的个人电脑，通常重达1至3公斤。最早商业化销售的现代笔记本电脑是PowerBook 100。[来源请求]此前的世界第一台便携式电脑Macintosh Portable体形巨大，并不受消费者欢迎。现在的发展趋势是体积越来越小，重量越来越轻，而功能却越发强大。为了缩小体积，笔记型电脑通常拥有液晶显示器（液晶屏），现在新型的部分机种甚至有触屏。除了键盘以外，还装有触摸板（touchpad）或触控点作为定位设备（Pointing device）。

Figure 2: Naturally annotated resources.

To expand the seed dictionary, the items with high confidence in the term translation candidate list will be selected as incremental dictionary items. By doing this, we can make up for the seed dictionary as the growth of term pairs.

2.4 Probability Learner

In order to substantially improve the quality of term and sentence translation, in this paper, we design a probability learner to generate the term translation table with probabilities in cooperating with SMT decoders. The probability learner combines word alignment model with the detected boundary candidates to generate the final term translation table. And the process of searching for the best boundary, c_i, can be formulated as the joint model:

$$i = \underset{1 \le i \le n}{\operatorname{argmax}}\, p(c_i)^{\lambda_5} \times p(c_i \dots c_n|e)^{\lambda_6} \times p(e|c_i \dots c_n)^{\lambda_7} \tag{8}$$

where $p(c_i \dots c_n|e)$ and $p(e|c_i \dots c_n)$ are word alignment probabilities of the source term and the target term, and $e = e_1 \dots e_m$.

In Example 1, $s =$ "所以 只能 使用 进程 间 通讯 (interprocess communication , IPC)". For the source term "interprocess communication", $c_1 =$ "所以", $c_2 =$ "只能", $c_3 =$ "使用", $c_4 =$ "进程", $c_5 =$ "间", $c_6 =$ "通讯", $e_1 =$ "interprocess", $e_2 =$ "communication". And the left boundary is incorrectly recognized by our baseline system as c_5, namely, the target term is $c_5c_6 =$"间 通讯". In order to correct the detection error, we enlarge or shrink the anchor from the left boundary to re-generate target terms, including the correct target term $c_4c_5c_6 =$"进程 间 通讯". Then, we select a best regenerated term which maximizes the joint probability according to Equation 8. In this work, the HMM-based word alignment model (Vogel et al., 1996) is employed to align words.

Next, we can extract term translation rules using the selected term above, and generate the term translation table as shown in Example 2. In Example 2, fields of the line "communication ||| 通信 ||| 0.387201 0.358436 0.623309 0.668845 ||| 0-0" includes 7 properties: source term, target term, phrase translation probability, lexical weights, inverse phrase translation probability, inverse lexical weights, word alignment.

In this paper, the default values of λ_5, λ_6 and λ_7 are set to 0.4, 0.3 and 0.3, respectively.

3 Experiments

We conduct the experiments to test the performance of our proposed framework on improving the quality of term and sentence translation. We will check how much improvement the proposed framework can achieve on the final MT results. The performance of term pair extraction is evaluated by precision (P); the quality of term translation and sentence translation are evaluated by precision (P) and BLEU, respectively.

3.1 Experimental Setup

All the experiments are conducted on our in-house developed MT toolkit which has a typical phrase-based decoder (Xiong et al., 2006) and a series of tools, including word alignment and phrase table extraction.

We test our method on English-to-Chinese translation in the field of software localization. The training data (1,199,589 sentences) and annotated test data (1,100 sentences) are taken from Microsoft Translation Memory, which is a domain-specific dataset. And additional data employed by this paper includes: the seed dictionary (102,308 source words[2], 24,094 terms from Mi-

[2]http://www.mdbg.net/chindict/chindict.php?page=cc-cedict

Source	Target
Mihr-Ohrmazd	拂多诞
Wicca	威卡尔
Francis Dashwood	弗朗西斯达希武德
Religious Studies	宗教学
Introduction to the Science of Religion	宗教科学引论
History of Religions	宗教史学
Phenomenology of Religion	宗教现象学
anomalous monism	无法则一元论
qualia	感质
Panspermia	泛种论
Determinism	决定论

Table 1: Extracted English-Chinese term translation candidates

crosoft Terminology Collection), Chinese Pinyin table (7,809 Chinese characters[3]). The gold standard of term translation of test data are human annotated.

All the MT systems are tuned by the development set (1,000 sentences) using ZMERT (Zaidan, 2009) with the objective to optimize BLEU (Papineni et al., 2002). The higher the BLEU score, the better the translation is. And the statistical significance test is performed by the re-sampling approach (Koehn, 2004).

3.2 Results and Analysis

(1) The Term Extraction Tests

Firstly, we will evaluate the extraction performance of term translation candidates. In our experiments, the focused crawler has downloaded 162,543,832 web pages. And there are 12,673,286 pages that contain 49,976,931 parenthesized sentences selected by the parenthesized sentence filter in total.

The baseline term extraction system is denoted as "Baseline" which is implemented according to the work introduced by (Cao et al., 2007). The baseline system has extracted 10,823,132 terms from above web pages. And our system, being denoted as "TermExt", outputs 12,048,310 terms. As we can see, the **recall** has been increased by 11.32% using our proposed framework.

Then, We sample the extracted terms 10 times on the baseline system and the proposed framework, respectively. And each sample includes 1,000 terms. And we report the average precision in Table 2.

[3]http://www.51windows.net/pages/gb2312.htm

In contrast to the baseline approach, the figures in Table 2 show that the **precision** of Chinese terms has been increased by 2.9 points, and the **precision** of term pairs has been increased by 4.1 points. Thus, according to the bold figures in Table 2, we can draw a conclusion that term extraction can be substantially increased by the proposed framework.

(2) The SMT Translation Tests

Secondly, we test whether the proposed framework can further improve the performance of term and sentence translation, compared with the baseline system. The strong baseline system, e.g., well tuned Moses, is denoted as "Moses". And our SMT system is denoted as "MaxEntSMT". The translation results based on the extracted term dictionary are labeled with "MaxEntSMT+BaselineDict" and "MaxEntSMT+TermExtDict", respectively. Correspondingly, the translation results based on the term translation table are labeled with "MaxEntSMT+TermExtTable". The word alignment was conducted bidirectionally and then symmetrized for extracting phrases as Moses (Koehn et al., 2007) does. The test set includes 1,100 sentences with 1,208 bilingual term pairs altogether. In order to highlight the performance of term translation, we count the number of terms that are translated exactly correctly, and the corresponding term translation results are denoted as "Term (P/%)" (exactly matching). Meanwhile, the sentence translation results are labeled "Sentence (BLEU/%)". We report all the results in Table 3.

In Table 3, our in-house developed SMT system makes the translation result worse than Moses.

	Number of Terms	Chinese Terms (P/%)	Term Pairs (P%)
Baseline	10,823,132	94.30	88.20
TermExt	12,048,310	**97.20****	**92.30****

"**" means the scores are significantly better than previous lines with $p < 0.01$.

Table 2: The performance of term extraction

	Term (P/%)	Sentence (BLEU/%)
Moses	86.43	46.01
MaxEntSMT	86.14	45.93
MaxEntSMT+BaselineDict	89.47	46.19
MaxEntSMT+TermExtDict	91.22	46.35
MaxEntSMT+TermExtTable	**94.38****	**47.26****

"**" means the scores are significantly better than previous lines with $p < 0.01$.

Table 3: The performance of translation

However, with the help of the proposed framework, the term translation quality is significantly improved by more than 7.95% accuracy. Non-term words are also strongly improved by the framework, because that the accuracy ratio of term words translation has been much improved and fewer non-term words are translated incorrectly. In sentence translation, the bold figures in Table 3 demonstrate that it improves the translation quality by 1.25 absolute BLEU points, compared with the well tuned Moses. Considering one term on average in a single sentence in the test set, the BLEU scores are very promising actually, and our goals on term translation have been achieved.

In summary, we can draw the conclusion that the proposed term extraction framework significantly improves the performance of term extraction from web pages, and further substantially improves the performance of MT in term of term translation and sentence translation.

4 Related Work

For term translation pairs extraction from parenthetical sentences, Cao *et al.*(Cao et al., 2007) and Lin *et al.*, like us, proposed two different methods to mine bilingual dictionaries. Cao *et al.* used a 300GB collection of web documents as input. They extracted candidate translations using predefined templates, and used supervised learning to build models that deal with phonetic transliterations and semantic translations separately. Lin *et al.* used a word alignment algorithm, not to make a distinction between translations and transliterations, to identify the terms being translated relying on unsupervised learning.

Our work depends on supervised learning with naturally annotated resources (e.g., Wikipedia) to train a term recognization model and detect left boundary candidates of a term. In addition, our method combines word alignment model with the detected boundary candidates to generate the final term translation table with probabilities for MT, rather than the extracted bilingual term dictionary. We make no distinction between translations and transliterations.

5 Conclusion

In this paper, we have presented an simple, straightforward and effective framework to learn from parenthetical sentences for term translation in MT. The proposed framework continuously extracts term translation candidates from parenthetical sentences from web pages, generates the term translation table, then regards the term translation table as a feature of MT decoders, finally substantially boosts term translation and sentence translation. The experimental results are promising.

References

Khurshid Ahmad, Lee Gillam, and Lena Tostevin. 2000. Weirdness indexing for logical document extrapolation and retrieval. In *Proceedings of the Eighth Text Retrieval Conference (TREC-8)*.

Guihong Cao, Jianfeng Gao, Jian-Yun Nie, and WA Redmond. 2007. A system to mine large-scale bilingual dictionaries from monolingual web. *Proceedings of MT Summit XI*, pages 57–64.

Jonathan D. Cohen. 1995. Highlights: Language- and domain-independent automatic indexing terms for abstracting. *Journal of the American Society for Information Science*, 46(3):162–174.

David A. Evans and Robert G. Lefferts. 1995. Clarittrec experiments. *Information Processing and Management*, 31(3):385–395.

Katerina Frantzi, Sophia Ananiadou, and Hideki Mima. 2000. Automatic recognition of multi-word terms: the c-value/nc-value method. *International Journal on Digital Libraries*, 3(2):115–130.

Philipp Koehn. 2004. Statistical significance tests for machine translation evaluation. In *Proceedings of EMNLP 2004*.

Philipp Koehn, Hieu Hoang, Alexandra Birch, Chris Callison-Burch, Marcello Federico, Nicola Bertoldi, Brooke Cowan, Wade Shen, Christine Moran, and Richard Zens. 2007. Moses: open source toolkit for statistical machine translation. In *Proceedings of ACL 2007*.

Ronald N. Kostoff, Joel A. Block, Jeffrey L. Solka, Michael B. Briggs, Robert L. Rushenberg, Jesse A. Stump, Dustin Johnson, Terence J. Lyons, and Jeffrey R. Wyatt. 2009. Literature-related discovery. *Annual Review of Information Science and Technology*, 43(1):171.

L Kozakov, Y. Park, T. H. Fin, Y. Drissi, Y N Doganata, and T. Cofino. 2004. Glossary extraction and knowledge in large organisations via semantic web technologies. In *Proceedings of the 6th International Semantic Web Conference and the 2nd Asian Semantic Web Conference*.

Els Lefever, Lieve Macken, and Veronique Hoste. 2009. Language-independent bilingual terminology extraction from a multilingual parallel corpus. In *Proceedings of EACL 2009*.

Olena Medelyan and Ian H. Witten. 2006. Thesaurus based automatic keyphrase indexing. In *Proceedings of the ACM/IEEE-CS Joint Conference on Digital Libraries*.

Anshika Pal, Deepak Singh Tomar, and SC Shrivastava. 2009. Effective focused crawling based on content and link structure analysis. *arXiv preprint arXiv:0906.5034*.

Kishore Papineni, Salim Roukos, Todd Ward, and Wei-jing Zhu. 2002. Bleu: a method for automatic evaluation of machine translation. In *Proceedings of ACL 2002*.

Youngia Park, Roy J Byrd, and Branimir K Boguraev. 2002. Automatic glossary extraction: beyond terminology identification. In *Proceedings of COLING 2002*.

Feiliang Ren, Jingbo Zhu, and Huizhen Wang. 2010. Web-based technical term translation pairs mining for patent document translation. In *Proceedings of the 6th International Conference on Natural Language Processing and Knowledge Engineering (NLP-KE 2010)*.

F. Sclano and P. Velardi. 2007. Termextractor: a web application to learn the shared terminology of emergent web communities. In *Proceedings of the 3rd International Conference on Interoperability for Enterprise Software and Applications (I-ESA 2007)*.

Stephan Vogel, Hermann Ney, and Christoph Tillmann. 1996. Hmm-based word alignment in statistical translation. In *Proceedings of the 16th conference on Computational linguistics*, volume 2, pages 836–841.

Deyi Xiong, Qun Liu, and Shouxun Lin. 2006. Maximum entropy based phrase reordering model for statistical machine translation. In *proceedings of COLING-ACL 2006*.

Omar F. Zaidan. 2009. Z-mert: A fully configurable open source tool for minimum error rate training of machine translation systems. *The Prague Bulletin of Mathematical Linguistics*, 91:79–88.

Ziqi Zhang, J. Iria, and Christopher Brewster. 2008. A comparative evaluation of term recognition algorithms. In *LREC 2008*.

Zili Zhou, Yanna Wang, and Junzhong Gu. 2008. Markov-based automatic term extraction. In *Future BioMedical Information Engineering, 2008*.

Author Index

Association for Computational Linguistics
209 N. Eighth Street
Stroudsburg, Pennsylvania 18360

CURRAN ASSOCIATES INC.
proceedings.com

ISBN 978-1-5108-5289-1

9 781510 852891